S0-BRJ-320

Local Area
Networks
in Libraries

Supplements to
COMPUTERS IN LIBRARIES

1. Essential Guide to dBase III+ in Libraries
   Karl Beiser
   ISBN 0-88736-064-5   1987
2. Essential Guide to Bulletin Board Systems
   Patrick R. Dewey
   ISBN 0-88736-066-1   1987
3. Microcomputers for the Online Searcher
   Ralph Alberico
   ISBN 0-88736-093-9   1987
4. Printers for Use with OCLC Workstations
   James Speed Hensinger
   ISBN 0-88736-180-3   1987
5. Developing Microcomputer Work Areas in Academic Libraries
   Jeannine Uppgard
   ISBN 0-88736-233-8   1988
6. Microcomputers and the Reference Librarian
   Patrick R. Dewey
   ISBN 0-88736-234-6   1988
7. Retrospective Conversion: A Practical Guide for Libraries
   Jane Beaumont and Joseph P. Cox
   ISBN 0-88736-352-0   1988
8. Connecting with Technology 1988: Microcomputers in Libraries
   Nancy Melin Nelson, ed.
   ISBN 0-88736-330-X   1989
9. The Macintosh ® Press: Desktop Publishing for Libraries
   Richard D. Johnson and Harriett H. Johnson
   ISBN 0-88736-287-7   1989
10. Expert Systems for Reference and Information Retrieval
    Ralph Alberico and Mary Micco
    ISBN 0-88736-232-X   1990
11. EMail for Libraries
    Patrick R. Dewey
    ISBN 0-88736-327-X   1989
12. 101 Uses of dBase in Libraries
    Lynne Hayman, ed.
    ISBN 0-88736-427-6   1990
13. FAX for Libraries
    Patrick R. Dewey
    ISBN 0-88736-480-2   1990
14. The Librarian's Guide to WordPerfect 5.0
    Cynthia LaPier
    ISBN 0-88736-493-4   1990
15. Technology for the 90's
    Nancy Melin Nelson, ed.
    ISBN 0-88736-487-X   1990
16. Microcomputer Management and Maintenance for Libraries
    Elizabeth S. Lane
    ISBN 0-88736-522-1   1990
17. Public Access CD-ROMS in Libraries: Case Studies
    Linda Stewart, Kathy Chiang, and Bill Coons, eds.
    ISBN 0-88736-516-7   1990
18. The Systems Librarian Guide to Computers
    Michael Schuyler and Elliott Swanson
    ISBN 0-88736-580-9   1990
19. Essential Guide to dBase IV in Libraries
    Karl Beiser
    ISBN 0-88736-530-2   1991
20. UNIX and Libraries
    D. Scott Brandt
    ISBN 0-88736-541-8   1991
21. Integrated Online Library Catalogs
    Jennifer Cargill, ed.
    ISBN 0-88736-675-9   1990
22. CD-ROM Retrieval Software: An Overview
    Blaine Victor Morrow
    ISBN 0-88736-667-8   1991
23. CD-ROM Licensing and Copyright Issues for Libraries
    Meta Nissley and Nancy Melin Nelson, editors
    ISBN 0-88736-701-1   1990

24. CD-ROM Local Area Networks: A User's Guide
    Norman Desmarais, ed.
    ISBN 0-88736-700-3   1991
25. Library Technology 1970-1990:
    Shaping the Library of the Future
    Nancy Melin Nelson, ed.
    ISBN 0-88736-695-3   1991
26. Library Technology for Visually and
    Physically Handicapped Patrons
    Barbara T. Mates
    ISBN 0-88736-704-6   1991
27. Local Area Networks in Libraries
    Kenneth Marks and Steven Nielsen
    ISBN 0-88736-705-4   1991
28. Small Project Automation for Libraries and
    Information Centers
    Jane Mandelbaum
    ISBN 0-88736-731-3   1991
29. Text Management for Libraries and Information Centers:
    Tools and Techniques
    Erwin K. Welsch and Kurt F. Welsch
    ISBN 0-88736-737-2   1992
30. Library Systems Migration: Changing Automated Systems
    in Libraries and Information Centers
    Gary M. Pitkin, ed.
    ISBN 0-88736-738-0   1991
31. From A - Z39.50: A Networking Primer
    James J. Michael
    ISBN 0-88736-766-6   1992
32. Search Sheets for OPACs on the Internet
    Marcia Henry, Linda Keenan, Michael Reagan
    ISBN 0-88736-767-4   1991
33. Directory of Directories on the Internet
    Ray Metz
    ISBN 0-88736-768-2   1991
34. Building Blocks for the National Network:
    Initiatives and Individuals
    Nancy Melin Nelson
    ISBN 0-88736-769-0   1991
35. Public Institutions: Capitalizing on the Internet
    Charles Worsley
    ISBN 0-88736-770-4   1991
36. A Directory of Computer Conferencing for Libraries
    Brian Williams
    ISBN 0-88736-771-2   1991
37. Optical Character Recognition: A Librarian's Guide
    Marlene Ogg and Harold Ogg
    ISBN 0-88736-778-X   1992
38. CD-ROM Research Collections
    Pat Ensor
    ISBN 0-88736-779-8   1992
39. Library LANs: Case Studies in Practice and Application
    Marshall Breeding
    ISBN 0-88736-786-0   1992
40. 101 Uses of Spreadsheets in Libraries
    Robert Mach alow
    ISBN 0-88736-791-7   1992
41. Library Computing in Canada: Bilingualism,
    Multiculturalism,
    and Transborder Connections
    Nancy Melin Nelson and Eric Flower, eds.
    ISBN 0-88736-792-5   1991
42. CD-ROM in Libraries: A Reader
    Meta Nissley, ed.
    ISBN 0-88736-800-X   1992
43. Automating the Library with AskSam:
    A Practical Handbook
    Marcia D. Talley and Virginia A. McNitt
    ISBN 0-88736-801-8   1991

Local Area

Networks

in Libraries

76613

Kenneth E. Marks and Steven P. Nielsen

Meckler
Westport • London

Library of Congress Cataloging-in-Publication Data

Marks, Kenneth E., 1945 -
    Local area networks in libraries / Kenneth E. Marks and Steven P.
Nielsen.
        p.   cm.   -- (Supplements to Computers in libraries)
    Includes bibliographical references and index.
    ISBN 0-88736-705-4 : $
    1. Local area networks (Computer networks)--Library applications.
2. Library information networks. 3. Libraries--Automation.
I. Nielsen, Steven P.   II. Title.   III. Series.
Z678.93.L63M37   1991
021.6'5--dc20   91-8501
                                                       CIP

British Library Cataloguing-in-Publication Data

Marks, Kenneth E.
    Local area networks in libraries.
    - (Computers in libraries)
    I. Title   II. Nielsen, Steven P.   III. Series
    025.04

    ISBN 0-88736-705-4

Meckler Publishing, the publishing division of Meckler Corporation,
    11 Ferry Lane West, Westport, CT 06880.
Meckler Ltd., 247-249 Vauxhall Bridge Road,
    London SW1V 1HQ, U.K.

Printed on acid free paper.
Printed and bound in the United States of America.

Contents

Preface

Five years ago, the authors began a collaboration that let them explore the application of electronic technologies in a library environment. One author was the university librarian and the other the fiscal officer. The organization that provided the testbed for the exploration and testing of various technologies, hardware, and software applications was the Merrill Library and Learning Resources Program (MLLRP), Utah State University. More than the traditional library was involved in this program. Early in the 1970s the university library, telecommunications (radio, television, and supporting engineering services), and publication design and production (printing, editorial, graphics, and photography) were brought together to form an organization to support students and faculty in the teaching, learning, research, and public services activities of the institution. The organization was created fifteen years before the technologies became available to support the achievement of institutional goals.

The mid-eighties witnessed the development of a variety of technologies that offered the prospect of assisting MLLRP in fulfilling its mission. Among those technologies was local area networking and the personal computer. These extended the possibility of bringing together in an integrated fashion the activities of the disparate parts of the MLLRP organization.

The reader should not conclude from the preceding statements that the organization had not embraced automation and telecommunications technologies as they were introduced to the marketplace. Integrated library systems, the national library network (OCLC), online database searching, the telecommunication of text for processing by typesetters, and electronic graphics in the television environment were all in use. There was a fundamental problem, however, because none of these activities could be integrated in one system that permitted MLLRP staff to share equipment and resources or utilize common databases.

The emergence of local area networking in the early 1980s seemed to the authors to offer the possibility of aiding MLLRP in capitalizing on its wide range of resources to deliver improved and more cost-effective services to campus clientele. The first efforts at networking were tentative and limited involving only the administrative office and three networked personal computers and supporting printers. Although the first networking effort involved an ARCNET network, a choice was made very early in our work to move to NOVELL network operating system software. We were convinced that for our environment and requirements, this set of network products was best for us. We have utilized every version of NOVELL software from Netware 2.0 to Netware 386 and eagerly wait for future versions. Our experience with NOVELL technical support has been uniformly good. Within the university community we have had the opportunity to acquire the software at substantially discounted prices which has made budget justification significantly easier.

To say that our experience with local area networking has been character building would understate the case. We have experienced both the agony and frustration of network failure and incompatibility as well as the pleasure of improved organizational communication and the successful delivery of new services within the library and to the campus. Especially in the first two or three years of our experience, there were no road maps to chart the way for us or groups that we could contact for assistance. That situation is gradually changing as special interest groups have formed within a number of the professional library associations. Still there is an enormous gap in the employment of local area networks in the library community.

Those libraries that are large enough by themselves or part of larger organizations, such as a university, a large municipality, or corporation, may have the personnel available to facilitate the move to and use of local area networking. But too many libraries are not quite large enough to quickly take on the process of moving to a local area networked environment. These libraries should make every effort to seize the opportunity to utilize local area networks. Begin small, progress in limited measured steps, and keep clearly in mind the goals and purposes that have been identified for the local area network.

The authors offer this work based on their experience in local area networking in the library environment. We have suffered through an endless number of mistakes that, perhaps, through this book, we can help other librarians avoid. The book is not intended to be exhaustive in its examination or coverage of the topic of local area networking in libraries. That would be an impossible assignment for the territory is constantly changing. We believe the general process of moving from consideration of a local area network, through the design and implementation, and ultimately to the operation of a local area network, can be sketched and discussed. This work is not a "how-to-do-it" manual that offers a series of rote steps that might be employed to move to local area networking. The authors offer a more generalized review of the sequence of activities that might come into play as librarians consider local area networking. The idiosyncracies and unique conditions of each library will finally dictate the steps that can be most effectively utilized.

Many librarians already involved extensively in the use of automation and telecommunications in their libraries can be lured into complacency about local area networking thinking their earlier experiences will protect them. While some protection can be gained, local area networking opens up a raft of new concerns, technical problems, and organizational challenges that must be addressed if it is to make a successful contribution to a library's goals.

There are numerous individuals who have contributed to the writing of this book. The MLLRP staff of Utah State University, personnel at Novell, and the owner, Tony Loosle, of The Computer Station in Logan, Utah, have supplied the fodder for daily experiences and the advice and counsel from which this book is drawn. Special appreciation is expressed to Leo Harris, Frances Bradburn, and Gary Weathersbee who reviewed the text offering uninhibited advice and counsel. The degree to which that advice and counsel were taken is the full responsibility of the authors as is the accuracy of the entire text.

One of the authors will be reaffirming the accuracy of the text personally by using it to assist in the local area networking of another academic library with which he has just become affiliated. The Joyner Library faculty and staff at East Carolina University are embarking on a project that will change not only the way in which they work but the organization of which they are members.

Finally, both authors express amazement at the tolerance and forbearance their spouses and families have displayed during the production of this volume. We believe local area networking can be an addictive experience and warn readers of that possibility. Once you have begun local area networking there is no turning back; the way in which your library operates and you work will change fundamentally.

Introduction

What are the reasons for local area networking in libraries? There are at least two ways to approach this question. One way is to look at the library as a self-contained organization; the other considers the library in its role as a member of a larger organization and the complex information infrastructure that is emerging not only in the United States but the entire world. A sufficient rationale for engaging in local area networking can be found in either view.

Within the context of a self-contained organization, local area networking can offer a variety of benefits to a library. Some of these will be influenced by the size of the library, its budget, the size of its staff, and the range of automation experience the library staff already has. Local area networking may permit the small library with a small staff and a limited budget to expand its limited use of automation, that is, a circulation system, to include a public access online catalog and word processing and spreadsheet use by library staff. The larger library may be able to realize a substantial savings in equipment by eliminating the need for individual terminals, each of which has its own use. A library using an integrated library system may discover that it can interface with Ethernet networks, creating the opportunity to make the online catalog and CD-ROM products accessible from the same terminal. Substituting personal computers for the dumb terminal of an integrated library system may provide another avenue for savings in equipment costs as well as maintenance and repair costs. Additionally, purchasing software licenses can often result in a substantial savings compared with the investment in individual copies of a software application.

The savings listed in the preceding paragraph can often be realized immediately as a local area network becomes operational. There are longer-term economies that occur as library staff are trained and brought into the network environment. Quantifying the savings or cost avoidance may be more difficult as a library staff becomes skilled in using electronic mail. Calendars, scheduling equipment and facilities, and groupware applications can enhance the productivity of library staff on an individual as well as organizational basis.

Remote access by patrons to a library's local area network may initially focus on being able to query the online catalog. Quickly, library staff should be capitalizing on the opportunities for mounting a variety of locally developed databases ranging from library-specific information to community-based information resources. There is enormous potential for libraries in extending access to community- or campus-wide information systems (CWIS). Local calendars, local news of interest, local transportation schedules, weather forecasts, and such, are types of information that can be made broadly available in a network environment.

Networking--local, metropolitan, or wide area--is becoming increasingly common among organizations and institutions of all types and sizes. Since most libraries are affiliated with a larger organization, it will be important for libraries to be an integral part of the organization-wide communication infrastructure. Any part of the organization that remains outside of this infrastructure may be largely excluded from the formal and informal decision-making systems that are constantly in flux.

Although the early manifestations of local area networking have occurred within higher education, and more specifically the research institutions, the growing movement to create the National Research and Education Network has implications for nearly all libraries. Access to this national, and by association, international information system network will be through a series of regional, state, and local networks. Gateway access from a local area network will be both the logical and legitimate route to these "superhighways" of data and information. The inability to access these national and international networks will certainly complicate the issue of equality of access to information. Perhaps the critical consideration to keep in mind is that the smallest library in a networked environment has the potential, through gateways, to access, use, and contribute to the broader information community.

While it can be argued that networking is inevitable for libraries, the final decision must rest with each library. The decision can be made unilaterally by library administrators, but that may be a recipe for disaster. Although in most instances library staff will be using services available on the local area network, those staff members should have an understanding of the range of library and individual commitments that will have to be made if the local area network is to be successful. Technical understanding is not a necessity, although it is helpful if library staff have a basic understanding of the technology employed. It is crucial that library staff comprehend the process required to bring a network to operational status and the work required to maintain the system. If so, expectations will certainly be more realistic and the possibility of disillusionment significantly diminished.

Those libraries that do make the commitment to engage in local area networking will focus initially on the four basic applications that are facilitated in this environment: word processing, spreadsheets, databases, and communications. Obviously, there is enough in these four areas to keep most library staff occupied for a long period of time. But there is also a need to look beyond the immediate gain and the computing model of networking to the fast approaching multimedia-based computing environment that can expand the horizons of networking in totally different directions.

1

LAN Technology

Local area networking is a relative newcomer to the world of computing, experiencing phenomenal growth in the last five years. The impetus for local area networking received its principal focus when Xerox, Digital, and Intel introduced Ethernet to the computing world around 1980. The origins of local area networks can be traced to the original work done in the late 1960s under the auspices of the Department of Defense that resulted in the creation of Arpanet.

LAN Characteristics

It is important to understand the characteristics of a local area network that distinguish it from two other forms of networking: metropolitan and wide area. The easiest way to approach this task may be to list those differentiating qualities of a local area network, comment upon them, and then discuss them in relation to both the metropolitan and wide area network.

There seem to be three commonly accepted characteristics of a local area network. First, a local area network is very limited geographically: an office, a floor in a building, an entire building, or a "campus." Second, data transmission is considered high speed, in the range of 10 MBPS. Third, data transmission occurs over a common medium.

A metropolitan area network typically encompasses a larger geographical area, as the name indicates a city or possibly a geographic region. The wide area network (WAN) is used to link installations on a national or international basis. The WAN typically uses T-1 transmission capabilities which function at 1.544 MBPS. WANs also make use of packet switching in transmitting information.

While there are three fundamental characteristics of a local area network, there are a number of benefits of local area networking that are often confused with some of the additional characteristics attributed to local area networking. A listing of both of these follows because they provide an understanding of why organizations and individuals have adopted local area networking with such enthusiasm. We draw from other sources for these lists. General characteristics consist of:[1]

- high data rates (typically 1 to 10 MBPS)
- limited geographical scope--typically spanning about 1 kilometer
- support of full connectivity--all devices should have the potential to communicate with each other
- equal access by all user devices
- ease of reconfiguration and maintenance
- good reliability and error characteristics
- stability under high load
- compatibility to the greatest extent possible to a variety of equipment
- relatively low cost

The benefits are as follows:[2]

- Costly peripherals such as laser printers, hard disks, and modems can be shared by all users of a LAN.
- Information too can be shared; for example, all members of an office can use their own PCs to access and update an important database.
- Another plus is electronic mail--using PCs to send and receive interoffice messages. Some LANs allow PCs to link up with minicomputers, mainframes, and even computer networks in other locations.
- For management, LANs represent a way to increase productivity with a modest outlay. Usually, PCs have already been purchased for the office; a LAN makes their use more efficient.
- In addition, an office with a LAN requires fewer printers and hard disks.
- For those using PCs, a LAN can make work less frustrating-- fewer floppies to keep track of, easier access to files, and ready use of all hardware on the system.
- Work becomes less solitary--electronic mail makes it easier to work together with the people in your office.

The cost of the peripherals mentioned in this quote has dropped dramatically to be supplanted by other benefits. As important as any is access to the equipment necessary to ensure an adequate and timely backup of data found on the network and its nodes. Beyond the actual sharing of this backup equipment is the availability of a network administrator who can schedule and implement the actual process of backingup the entire network or limited portions.

Interfaces (either bridges or gateways) to other networks can be minimized reducing what might otherwise be an unacceptable hardware cost. Telecommunications costs may also be reduced.

Databases can be made more broadly available to the entire library facilitating access to information. As specialized local-interest databases are constructed for and by the library staff, it is possible to create customized front-ends that can enhance accessibility.

Local area networks present administrators with the opportunity to capitalize on an investment they have already made in personal computing equipment. The prospect of allowing employees to continue to use their personal computers for their own individual tasks while being linked to centralized data storage seems almost too good to be true. Often it *is* too good to be true because administrators and staff do not possess the necessary level of understanding of the strengths and weaknesses of local area networking.

The architecture of contemporary networking can assume many forms. While it is not common to have a mix of the traditional topologies in the same network, technologies change so quickly that implementation and modification of a local area network occur nearly simultaneously. The most important commitment that library administrators and network staff can establish is to make all network decisions in a way that ensures long-term compatibility.

LAN Architectures

There are, perhaps, three different LAN architectures or approaches to the way in which a network functions. These are peer-to-peer, client/server, and file server. Each of these has its respective strengths and weaknesses.

A peer-to-peer network has each computer on the network sharing designated data and resources with all other networked computers on an equal basis. This type of network is usually less costly to install and implement. If a library has a minimal number of workstations that need to be connected and limited funds, this option may be most satisfactory. Because each workstation functions as a server, there is usually no reason to purchase a separate server. But this type of network also has its drawbacks: it will often experience inconsistent transmission speeds; and if all of the other workstations are not turned on, the network will be "down."

The client/server network divides functions between a high-performance PC that stands as the server holding the files and application software, thereby relieving the other networked computers of certain tasks. The other PCs on the network can do other tasks more effectively. This network will always involve two pieces of software--the server software and the application that the client computer runs. Until recently, all of the processing occurred at the individual workstations, a fact often overlooked by network users. This approach permits a large hard disk to serve many users eliminating the need for hard disks on each workstation. The result is that a less expensive personal computer can be used for the workstation and maintaining and backingup files takes place more easily.

The file server network supplies a dedicated central computer or computers that function as central storage devices supporting the remaining computers on the network. This arrangement permits, with appropriate rights, file sharing among network users. If the users have large numbers of files to store and there is a need to share them, this configuration could be very effective. The most attractive feature of the file server-based network has thus far been its price.

It is important to remember that regardless of the network architecture employed, there are certain characteristics common to all. One is the capacity to share data. Another is the capacity to provide shared equipment resources to all members of the network.

A local area network consists of several distinctive components, such as nodes, links, servers, and NIC's. Each of these will be discussed briefly.

Nodes

The term node is simply another way of referring to a personal computer, terminal, or workstation that is part of a network. A node is a place where work on the network can be accomplished.

Links

Network links are the media used to connect the various nodes and peripherals to the network. The types of media that can be used as links will be discussed later in this chapter. Establishing the proper configuration of media for linking a network is one of the most important things to do before installing a local area network.

Servers

Servers are the heart of the local area network. The first distinction that should be made is between dedicated and non-dedicated. The dedicated server is a PC that may or may not have a monitor and keyboard and whose only function is to respond to the inquiries of other equipment on the network. A non-dedicated server is a PC that continues to function as a regular PC while it supplies services to the network.

The server is often the most difficult piece of equipment to sell to an organization that is embarking on local area networking because it is quite expensive and perceived as the least used part of the network. This latter perception can be disproved with a little study that will demonstrate the cost effectiveness of the server. A common error, usually committed through oversight, is the purchase of an expensive monitor to accompany the server.

If it is determined that a monitor is needed, be certain it is an inexpensive monochrome monitor since it will be used only to observe network performance.

As networks have become more complex and a wider range of activities have been placed on them, the types of servers available for network use have expanded. Initially, there were disk servers and file servers. A disk server simply provides a hard disk that is available to be used by any of the networked PCs. In essence each networked PC has an additional disk drive to use; in the case of diskless PCs, it gives them the same capability as PCs with hard disks. The individual PC takes information from the disk server, works with it on its own hard disk, and then, when it has completed the manipulation, returns the information to the disk server. Obviously, there is the potential for some significant problems when many PCs are competing for the opportunity to work with the information on the hard disk.

File servers minimize the individual PC's need for disk storage by providing centralized hard-disk storage. The file server accepts the request from the individual PC and processes the information on the hard disk using the file server's operating system. The file server does the work through its filing capabilities and internal database services.

Print servers provide network users with the opportunity to begin to minimize peripherals. Depending upon the size of a network, the print server can be a separate PC, but more often it is also the file server. Demand for printing on most networks will not normally cause any degradation in file access speeds. NOVELL Netware Fconsole command will permit a network administrator to monitor the actual use of the server which will facilitate the decision of whether or not a separate print server is needed. When a separate print server is justified, it will usually be able to take in printing faster than the printers can generate output. This is why print servers will have additional disk space or RAM to queue the jobs waiting for the printer. This process is known as print spooling.

Database servers are newcomers to local area networking and are

> ...far more specialized than file servers, database servers perform data retrieval and computation services for personal computers, and send back only results of database queries or confirmations of successful input.
>
> SQL is the most popular (and hyped) query language for database servers. SQL capabilities are usually embedded in the database languages (Dbase, for example), or can be added to more general-purpose languages, like C.[3]

It will probably be some time before most libraries develop the local area networking sophistication or the staff with programming skills or capabilities to make use of the potential that database servers can offer. This may change as more user-friendly access tools and front-ends become available.

Database servers may become one of the major factors in expanding the utilization of local area networks in libraries. The reality of not having to replicate a database many times to make it broadly available throughout a library can have an immediate impact on staff productivity, not to mention the more efficient use of time by library patrons. When heavily used local databases can be updated directly from several locations while patrons have uninterrupted access, database servers will have realized their potential.

Communications servers permit the sharing of modems, telefaxes, satellite transmissions, and gateways. The first two of these will be discussed in this section; gateways will be reviewed later in the chapter. There is no fundamental difference in the concept of a communications server whether a modem or a telefax is attached. Another aspect of communications servers must be anticipated, however. A communications server handles more than data going out; it also handles data coming into the local area network. This is an instance where the manner in which the network operating system handles remote computing becomes important. It is possible that the operating system will require the incoming inquiry to take over the operation of a PC on the local area network. It is equally possible that the incoming session will be required to take only a portion of the processing capacity that is available. Unless a local area network is large it is probably better to avoid a configuration that requires remote connections to take over local PCs completely.

As with database servers, there is a level of computer and network sophistication that must be present before these specialized servers are added to a local area network. The communications server, whether modem, fax, or both, is probably far more likely to be selected by most libraries because of the desire for remote access to other library databases and the need for quick communication among libraries. Fax servers have come a long way in a short time. There are fax servers that can be attached to a network that will notify a user when a message has been received so the person can call it up and read it. If the person desires a printed copy, the message can be routed as any other document would be to a network printer. Any person on the network can send faxes from their workstation, too. He or she must simply prepare the message to be sent using a word processing program, select the fax as the output, and identify the person the message is for. The fax server handles the rest of the task.

NICs

Network interface cards (NICs) are added to personal computers or workstations to allow them to attach to the network. There are a variety of cards available in the marketplace at widely varying prices. This can be one of the weak links in a network installation.

> Network interface cards (NICs) are the distinctive hardware component of local area neworks. Modems and mice use serial ports; printers use RS-232 or parallel ports; video displays use video boards; only LANs use NICs. NICs make possible the fast transmission speeds that make file servers, shared files and LAN operating systems feasible. NICs also determine what kind of cabling will be needed to tie the LAN together.[4]

Topology

Topology is the term used to describe the manner in which the network cable or media connect the workstations, terminals, and servers that comprise the network. Conversations with individuals involved with networking will quickly reveal that they are fervently committed to one or another topology. In fact, there are several considerations that should influence the decision regarding topology. Among them are the functional objectives of the local area network, the level of network reliability, the control strategy, and the operational costs of the local area network. The topology chosen will influence very directly the type of media used to connect the network and much of the cost of the local area network, so selecting the topology should be done with great care.

Any discussion of topology focuses on five choices. The reality of networking is such that, eventually, any network will be a hybrid of several of the topologies, regardless of what it may originally have used. The advantages and disadvantages of the peer-to-peer, star, bus, ring, and tree topologies will be discussed.

Peer-to-Peer

This is the simplest of all networks, linking two PCs together through their serial ports. The fact that there are only two PCs eliminates the need for addressing the computers. It is also secure because communications are restricted to the two computers unless the transmission media is tapped. Cost is minimized, too. But there are several disadvantages. First, other devices such as some mice and modems use the serial port on a PC. Second, communication through the serial port is very slow. Finally, while this type of network will permit the copying of files from one PC to another, direct access to the files on another PC or remote execution of an application on another PC may not be possible.

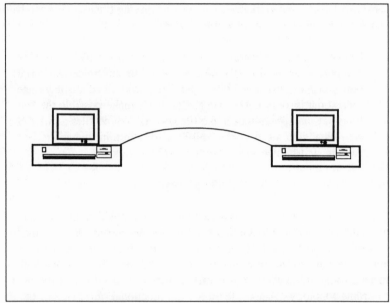

Figure 1. *Peer-to-Peer Topology. This is the simplest of all networks, linking two PCs together through their serial ports.*

Star

The star topology harks back to the mainframe environment where a centralized processor served the needs of distant terminals. It can be contended that the star configuration is not a true network since the individual nodes do not communicate directly with one another. The most distinguishing characteristic of the star topology is that all nodes are connected to a single hub or server. The result is that the central hub controls all routing of network traffic. The advantages of the star topology have been identified as:

- *Ease of servicing the network*. The presence of the central hub and other points of concentration such as wiring closets means service or reconfiguration of the network can be performed more easily.
- *One device/one connection*. The fact that each device in the star topology is connected directly to the central hub minimizes the impact of a failure of the connection. Regardless of the topology, connections are placed in a network that are most prone to failure. When a connection does fail, typically, only one node has to be disconnected to return the network to operation.

- *Centralized problem diagnosis.* Because the topology is based on a central hub, finding faults or problems in the network is far easier than in other topologies.
- *Simpler access protocols.* Because the connections are between a single node and the hub, there is no contention for use of the transmission medium. The result: access protocols are simpler.
- *Sharing of peripherals.* Equipment to be shared in the star topology must be near the central processor. This can make access to the peripherals easier and, if security is an issue, securing the equipment can be easier.

Disadvantages of the star topology are as follows:

- *Data transmission.* Transmission rates are slower since all communications have to be processed by the central hub before they can be sent on to their final destination.
- *Cable length.* The fact that each node is connected directly to the central hub results in large quantities of cabling being used. An associated problem results as cable trays and raceways fill up because of the quantity of cabling used.
- *Expandability.* The fact that a new node has to be connected to the central hub means that space has to be found in the conduit

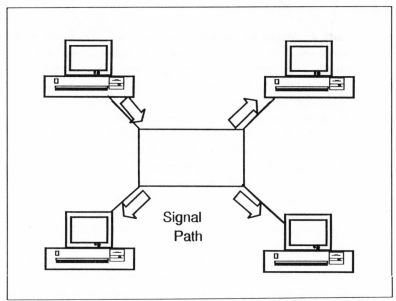

Figure 2. Star Bus Topology. The star bus has a centralized processor that serves the needs of the other terminals.

or raceways. Sometimes an organization will try to anticipate this situation by installing additional cable at the time of construction. The only problem is that it is impossible to forecast whether the cable will be the correct length.

- *Central node failure*. The most critical disadvantage of the star topology is the fact that when the central hub fails, the entire network fails. Unless there are dual central hubs installed, there is no way to guard against this failure.

The star topology has been heavily used in a wide variety of network installations, especially those that can make use of the twisted-pair media that is often found in great abundance in buildings. For smaller network configurations, star topology is a reasonable choice.

Bus

The most heavily used network topology may be the bus. A bus is single linear communications media (e.g., coaxial cable) that can begin at any location and end at any other location with each end having a terminator attached and each node connected by cable taps or similar devices. Certainly, ease of installing a bus and adding nodes to or removing nodes from a bus are influential when a topology is chosen. While much of its popularity may be due to the existence of Ethernet, the topology does have distinct advantages and disadvantages, which are listed by Tangney and O'Mahony.[5] The advantages are:

- *Short cable length and simple wiring layout*. Because there is a single common data path connecting all nodes, the bus topology allows a very short cable length to be used. This decreases the installation cost, and also leads to a simple, easy to maintain, wiring layout.
- *Resilient architecture*. The bus architecture has an inherent simplicity that makes it very reliable from a hardware point of view. There is a single cable through which all data propagates and to which all nodes are connected.
- *Easy to extend*. Additional nodes can be connected to an existing bus network at any point along its length. More extensive additions can be achieved by adding extra segments connected by a type of signal amplifier known as a repeater.

Some of the disadvantages are:

- *Fault diagnosis is difficult*. Although the simplicity of the bus topology means that there is very little to go wrong, fault

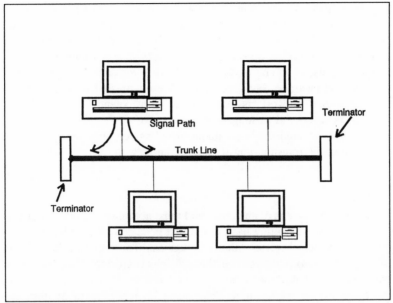

Figure 3. Linear Bus Topology. The bus may be the most heavily used network topology.

detection is not a simple matter. In most LANs based on a bus, control of the network is not centralized in any particular node. This means that detection of a fault may have to be performed from many points in the network.

- *Fault isolation is difficult.* In the star topology, a defective node can easily be isolated from the network by removing its connection at the center. If a node is faulty on a bus, it must be rectified at the point where the node is connected to the network. Once the fault has been located, the node can simply be removed. In the case where the fault is in the network medium itself, an entire segment of the bus must be disconnected.
- *Repeater configuration.* When a bus-type network has its backbone extended using repeaters, reconfiguration may be necessary. This may involve tailoring cable lengths, adjusting terminators, etc.
- *Nodes must be intelligent.* Each node on the network is directly connected to the central bus. This means that some way of deciding who can use the network at any given time must be performed in each node. It tends to increase the cost of the nodes irrespective of whether this is performed in hardware or software.

A few other characteristics of the bus topology deserve comment. Particular attention should be paid to the way in which messages are handled. First, all the devices connected to a bus can try to speak whenever they have a message to transmit. This results in a substantial level of contention for use of the network. Second, when messages are sent, all the nodes hear the messages but accept only those addressed to them. While extending a bus network is easy, there is a potential for problems. Expansion is successful as long as there is sensitivity to the length of the bus. Trying to expand the bus without installing repeaters will result in a degradation in the transmission of data on the network.

Ring

The ring topology is often considered to be nothing more than a bus that has the last node connecting back to the first node completing the ring configuration. In fact, there are other distinctions. The nodes in the ring are linked in a point-to-point fashion through which all transmissions on the network must pass until they reach their destination. Either separately or as part of the PC or workstation, there must be repeaters to amplify the transmission on its journey around the ring. Another consideration that has substantial implications, but which can be overlooked, is whether the ring is set up to be unidirectional or bidirectional.

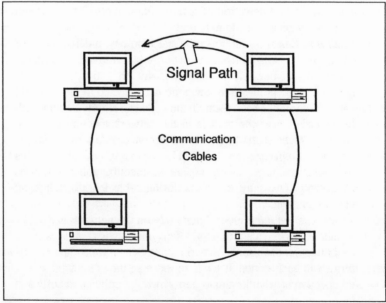

Figure 4. Ring Topology. The nodes in the ring are linked in a point-to-point fashion, connecting the last node to the first.

The unidirectional ring has the limitation of being able to send transmissions in only one route on the network, but there are some advantages to that situation. These are:

- Simple message routing.
- The sending node does not have to know the location of the receiving node, only its identifier.
- The investment required to set up the network is proportional to the number of nodes.
- Traffic on the ring can be higher since more than one message can be in transit at the same time.

The advantages and disadvantages generic to all rings have been identified by Tangney and O'Mahony.[6] The advantages of the ring are:

- *Short cable length.* The amount of cabling involved in a ring topology is comparable to that of a bus and is small relative to that of a star. This means that less connections will be needed, which will in turn increase network reliability.
- *No wiring closet space required.* Since there is only one cable connecting each node to its immediate neighbors, it is not necessary to allocate space in the building for wiring closets.
- *Suitable for optical fibers.* Using optical fibers offers the possibility of very high-speed transmission. Because traffic on a ring travels in one direction, it is easy to use optical fibers as a medium of transmission. Also, since a ring is made up of nodes connected by short segments of transmission medium, there is a possibility of mixing the types used for different parts of the network.

The disadvantages are:

- *Node failure causes network failure.* The transmission of data on a ring goes through *every* connected node on the ring before returning to the sender. If one node fails to pass data through itself, the entire network has failed and no traffic can flow until the defective node has been removed from the ring.
- *Difficult to diagnose faults.* The fact that failure of one node will affect all others has serious implications for fault diagnosis. It may be necessary to examine a series of adjacent nodes to determine the faulty one. This operation may also require diagnostic facilities to be built into each node.
- *Network reconfiguration is difficult.* The all or nothing nature of the ring topology can cause problems when one decides to extend

or modify the geographical scope of the network. It is not possible to shut down a small section of the ring while keeping the majority of it working normally.

- *Topology affects the access protocol.* Each node on a ring has a responsibility to pass on data that it receives. This means that the access protocol must take this into account. Before a node can transmit its own data, it must ensure that the medium is available for use.

Two other potential headaches with the ring topology involve the presence of repeaters. First, because the repeaters must be functional at all times on a ring, there is an increased probability of failure. Second, adding new repeaters to a ring to support added devices can be a substantial task in terms of determining its proper placement vis-a-vis existing repeaters on the ring.

Star Ring

This is a variation on the ring topology. In this configuration, a number of star hubs are made into nodes on the ring. Each star hub, in turn, connects to a star subnetwork.

Tree

The tree topology is a variation of the bus. Instead of just a single trunk there can be many branches off of the principal bus. In either configuration, data transmissions are sent throughout the entire network. The branches of a tree topology are created by using devices called splitters and repeaters. These are critical to the effective operation of the topology because they ensure that the electrical signal is properly transmitted over the media. Often, a tree will utilize a headend arrangement which functions as the common point of communication.

The existence of a headend device in a tree topology introduces the most significant disadvantage. If the headend fails, the network ceases functioning until the headend is repaired or replaced, not unlike the star topology. An advantage of the tree topology is the ease of expansion since a splitter can be added to create a new branch. It can be easier to locate problems, too, since entire branches can be disconnected from the network.

The topology chosen for a local area network will reflect a number of circumstances. The size of the network, the existence of media already in the building, the level of reliability, and other factors can influence the choice of topology. After a short while in operation, it is very likely that a network will have evolved into some hybrid arrangement that mirrors the changing needs of your library and its staff.

Another facet of local area networking, in addition to topologies, that people will debate endlessly is cabling or media. Often there are local circumstances that will short-circuit the debate about cabling, such as the existence of coaxial cable within a building or organization or the presence of a substantial amount of twisted-pair wiring in the walls of a library. In this case, it makes sense to take advantage of the existing wiring unless there is some overwhelming objection such as the level of interference that will affect the transmission of data.

Media

If there is the opportunity to cable a new facility, be certain that long-term needs are carefully analyzed. Remember a network will grow, the demands upon it will increase, and it will never be quite as inexpensive or easy to install additional cable as it is now. This may be the best justification for installing fiber optic cabling in a building. These points will be reviewed in greater detail later in the book, but they cannot be repeated or emphasized too often, because cabling is often the first thing cut from a new building when construction costs must be reduced.

Twisted Pair

Twisted-pair wiring is the ubiquitous wiring used for telephone systems that often seems to fill the walls and plenums of buildings. While there are two types of wiring, unshielded and shielded, they share many of the same characteristics. Perhaps most important to the organization installing a network, twisted-pair wiring is inexpensive and easy to handle. It is easy to splice, easy to connect, and easy to install. The tools required to work with twisted pair are simple and inexpensive as well. Twisted-pair wiring can be bent at right angles and stapled to walls or floors.

There is a fundamental problem with unshielded twisted-pair wiring that has limited its usefulness in many network environments: its susceptibility to interference. There are two types of interference that create particular problems: electromagnetic interference (EMI) and radio frequency interference (RFI). The sources of these types of interference are fluorescent lights, motors, elevators, and similar types of electrical equipment that would typically be found in most buildings. The effect of this interference is to degrade the transmission resulting in a drop in the quality of the data being sent over the network.

The response to this problem has been shielded twisted-pair wiring. The traditional twisted-pair wire is surrounded by another layer of insulation such as copper foil or wire braid that protects the wires, thus permitting data transmission without degradation in the signal. This is important because it allows shielded twisted pair to be used for more than just very low-speed network traffic.

Regardless of whether shielded or unshielded twisted pair is chosen, the value of installing a higher-quality variety of twisted pair, known as data grade medium, should be considered. This type of twisted pair attempts to minimize problems that could result from capacitance, resistance, and other differences in electrical characteristics of the cable.

Coaxial Cable

Although twisted-pair wiring may be the most pervasive cable in terms of its presence in a facility, one cannot assume it has been used most often to support local area networking. That honor may belong to coaxial cable, otherwise known as cable TV wiring. While it is not as inexpensive as twisted pair and not nearly as flexible, it does have a number of advantages that make it quite attractive as a wiring medium. It provides substantially greater bandwidth than twisted pair permitting more transmission channels to function simultaneously. It has significantly better resistance to noise or interference than twisted pair. It is constructed in a manner that offers the opportunity to avoid using conduit so it can be used in false flooring and ceilings more easily.

Coaxial cable is made up of two wires, an inner wire and an outer wire separated by an insulating material. Two types of coaxial cable are typically used in networking: one is the 50 ohm cable that is approximately three-eighths of an inch in diameter; the other is a 75 ohm cable that is nearly one-half inch in diameter. The 50 ohm cable is used in baseband LANs with relatively slow data transmission rates. The 75 ohm cable is used in broadband LANs offering the opportunity for large numbers of low-speed data channels as well as channels that can be used for higher-speed data transmission in addition to voice and video purposes.

Fiber

A relatively late arrival on the local area networking scene, fiber optic cable has been heralded as the answer to network cabling problems. This technology employs a thin glass or plastic strand to carry a beam of light from a light source that has converted the data to a digital format. There are two types of fiber optic cable, mono and multi-mode. The two types are presently incompatible because there is no way to connect them in a single system. While it does have a number of advantages, fiber optic cabling currently has an equal number of limitations. First and foremost of these is cost of the fiber. There is no question that, while its cost has dropped dramatically in the past two or three years, it is still several times more costly than coaxial cable or twisted-pair wiring. This is particularly the case when installation costs are calculated. Fiber optic cabling requires special tools for splicing and specifically trained individuals to perform the work of installing the media.

There is no question that fiber optic cable has a lower loss of signal resulting in the need for fewer repeaters or amplifiers to be installed in the network. Fiber optic cable is almost completely unaffected by noise or electrical interference. This is because fiber optic uses light rather than an electrical signal for transmitting data. Another advantage that fiber optic cable has is its level of security. In order to tap into the data transmission, the cable would have to be cut so a tap could be installed. This would result in network failure. Perhaps the greatest long-term advantage is the bandwidth of fiber optic cable. Since it is many times greater than either coaxial cable or twisted pair, it offers the promise of being able to transmit data in the form of images or video.

Other Media

There are a number of other approaches to the transmission media for local area networks. Microwave, infra-red, FM-radio, and ultrasonic transmissions have all been used in particular environments to support local area networking. Each of these has distinctive limitations and, in some situations, unique advantages. Any consideration of these possibilities would require the advice of a knowledgeable consultant or specialist.

Bandwidth

Any review of transmission media brings a person face-to-face with the questions of bandwidth and the terms baseband and broadband. "Bandwidth refers to the range of frequencies that can be accepted over an analog network, or the data rate in bits per second over a digital network. Bandwidth is a function of transmission medium and of the data modulation methods."[7]

Baseband transmission is a transmission technique that uses digital signals. It is simpler and less expensive than broadband because all of the network cable is used to send a single signal and the signal is sent on the network without any type of modification. While under most circumstances only one signal is sent on baseband transmission, it is possible to multiplex signals to send more than one. If there is concern about cost of the network, then baseband networks should be given consideration.

Broadband transmission works in a cable that contains many channels. Each of the channels can transmit data, voice, or video giving the network far greater potential. This capability requires network equipment that partitions the bandwidth that is available. The signal that is transmitted is an analog one.

Protocols

"The fundamental problem that network protocols solve is the sharing of a single wire--the network cable--among many workstations and servers, all of which may need to use it at any unpredictable time."[8] The two protocols used most often are token passing and carrier sense multiple access/collision detection (CSMA/CD). The token passing protocol is typical of the token ring network, and the CSMA/CD is commonly associated with the bus or tree topology. In terms of approach, the token passing protocol is very ordered in its method of permitting nodes on a network to transmit data. CSMA/CD uses an approach that can best be described as free-for-all or first-come-first-served.

While it is important that an individual involved in networking understand the distinctions, the choice of topology and other factors may make the selection of protocol a moot issue. There are also two other types of protocols involved in network operation, transport, and client/server. Explanations of their function in local area networking can be found in many books that address more technical issues related to networking.

Other Network Miscellany

Conventional wisdom states that all ventures into local area networking should begin with a small number of nodes and a limited area. The typical local area network, if it behaves as most do, will grow very quickly and, just as quickly, there will be a desire to introduce a wide variety of equipment that facilitate the network's growth and linkage with other networks and services. Each of these pieces of equipment that will be described can play an important part in the operation of a network, but it is important to understand the function each piece will contribute to the network. These will not be presented in any particular order.

Gateway

Gateway technology provides the means for a local area network to bridge or connect to other networks regardless of whether they are the same type or not, or mounted on mainframes or minicomputers. The connection can occur either locally or over long distances. If widely separated networks are connected a public data network such as Tymnet, Telenet or Compuserve may be used to make the link. One of the more common gateways in use is the X.25 gateway based on the CCITT standard x.25 packet switching protocol.

A gateway combines both hardware and software to accomplish its mission. It performs communications protocol conversion, network address translation, code conversion, and terminal emulation conversion. Gateways offer a migration path for the continued growth of a local area network as its users become more sophisticated and develop needs to communicate with other networks. This is an add-on to any local area network and will typically require someone with a fair degree of training to properly install and make operational. The move to add gateways to a local area network should occur only after the network has been stabilized and is functioning in an effective manner for some period of time.

Repeaters

This may be the least complicated network connecting device. The sole function of a repeater is to reamplify or regenerate a signal before passing it along the network. The presence of a repeater means that a network, such as a bus or tree, can be extended. It is important to remember that repeaters work only on the same type of cabling so a repeater could not connect networks using different media.

Bridges

After repeaters, bridges are probably the simplest piece of network equipment. Under most circumstances, a LAN administrator with some experience can install a bridge and bring it to operational status.

A bridge joins two physically separate but similar networks. For instance, two token ring or two bus networks could be joined together. It is conceivable that a token ring and a bus network could be joined together as long as they both were using the same communications protocol. Bridges can link networks using different media, enabling a fiber-based network to connect to a twisted-pair-based network. The result of two networks being bridged is that both networks function as if they belong to one large network with all of their respective nodes linked in a transparent manner. If a local area network grows too large due to the number of nodes or the traffic, it is possible to split the network into two separate local area networks that are connected by a bridge. Local performance on the two networks improves and the nodes on each of the networks can still communicate just as effectively as before.

Routers

As a local area network grows and is split into subnetworks or smaller networks, a point is reached where there may be more than one route that can be followed to transmit data from one node to another. This is where equipment known as routers enter networking. While a router may include all the functions found in a bridge, it performs a number of far more complicated tasks for the network.

A router must have extensive information about how the network is set up, how data packets are assembled, and how network addresses are established and assigned. This means that the individual who installs a router must have substantial network knowledge and training. It also means that routers are not normally added to a new network. Routers will examine each packet for its destination as it moves along the network and direct the packet to the appropriate node whether it is on the local system or on a distant network.

Brouters

If network needs are too complicated for a bridge but not sufficiently complex for a router to be installed, the brouter may be what is needed. In many ways, the brouter is just an intelligent bridge. In addition to the normal functions of a bridge, the brouter will take care of responding to the multiple path requirements of a network. As with the router, installing a brouter requires a high level of technical skill and that may mean using someone outside the library to do the installation.

OSI/ISO Standard

The successful development of local area networking has been dependent upon the acceptance of a number of standards related to the way in which communications can occur. One of the publicized standards is the OSI reference model. It was created to facilitate the development of new communications standards and to enable existing communications standards to identify their place in a total communications system.

A substantial literature has been written about the seven layers of the OSI reference model which the reader can explore to acquire an understanding of how the model is organized and how its parts relate. An important fact to remember is that many of the specialized pieces of networking equipment operate on specific layers of the model and presume an understanding of the layers and their relationship to one another.

NETBIOS

"Netbios is a low-level software interface that a program can use to communicate with network software on an IBM PC or compatible machine. Like the IBM PC's ROMBIOS it accepts commands from the program via special CPU instructions called software interrupts. Before making a NETBIOS call, the program creates and fills out a sort of electronic form called a Network Control Block (NCB). The NCB tells the network software which of the 19 Netbios functions is to be performed. It also contains other relevant information (for instance, the name of a system or program to receive some data). The program then 'submits' the form for processing by executing the software interrupt instruction."[9]

Most activities involving NETBIOS are handled invisibly by the Network Interface Card unless there is a reason to alter the interrupt configuration. This is more likely to be a problem with PC-based personal computers because the bus in them must connect all the individual parts of the PC. The bus has a limited number of interrupts that can be used. Prior to the advent of the newer ATs and high-powered accessories this was not a problem because there had been some degree of standardization on the type of equipment that would use each interrupt. This is no longer the case as more and more accessories are switchable. For example, if an NIC was added to an original IBM PC it is likely the default configuration would work. If the same NIC were added to a 386 machine with Super VGA, two serial ports, two LPT ports, and a mouse, it is likely that some experimenting will have to be done before the NIC is properly configured. There is a program (and there may be others) known as CHECKIT that identifies the interrupts available to use. Using this program in the set up mode can save a substantial amount of time and frustration.

LAN Marketplace

The local area network marketplace is a mirror of the entire microcomputing marketplace experiencing tremendous growth over the past several years. A large number of varied companies are competing for niches in the world of local area networking. Unquestionably, the largest producer of local area networking software is NOVELL, Inc. NOVELL, a market leader in the network world for the past several years, accounts for a significant percentage of the currently installed local area networks.

NOVELL has attempted to provide a range of products for all sizes of networks. Its systems range in size from two workstations to those that are virtually unlimited. The product that handles the smaller network is identified as ELS. It is currently marketed for up to 32 concurrent connections. ELS contains nearly all the functionality that larger network systems would have. This product offers a practical entry point into local area networking for the smaller library or the larger library that needs only a limited local area network installation. ELS installation is not difficult and the functionality provides basic networking services. It is easily upgraded to other versions of NOVELL network software if there is a need for network expansion at a later date.

NOVELL has two other network options currently on the market. One option is designed for the 286 computer and a newer product that utilizes the power of 386-based computers. As with other software companies, NOVELL numbers the versions of each product line as an effort to keep track of the changes in a software product. This can cause confusion. One way to minimize the confusion about versions of software is to complete and return the registration card that accompanies software packages. This will ensure that the company has the library's name and address so notices of new versions, updates, and upgrades will be received in a timely manner. Often the company will offer updates at a nominal fee. This will allow library staff the opportunity to remain current with changes in the software. There is a caution about moving to the newest software version too quickly. The newest version is not always best because radical modifications to the software do not always work as advertised. It may be better to wait for at least one revision of the upgrade to be released before moving to the upgrade.

The fact that NOVELL, Inc. has dominated the local area network marketplace for the past several years increases the likelihood that some version of NOVELL Netware may be selected by a library. This dominance is reflected in the existence of a large number of NOVELL user groups that have been created across the country to facilitate the sharing of experiences and knowledge that only comes from having worked with a piece of software for sometime. Although everyone talks about the importance of creating a written record of experience, fixes, solutions, and changes made to a network, most people become so consumed by the demands on their time that nothing is committed to paper or any permanent record. User groups provide a framework for sharing knowledge gained the hard way but willingly shared with others.

The authors have been actively involved in the networking of libraries for four years. Most of that time they have worked with the various iterations of NOVELL software. While the focus of this book is toward local area networking and libraries in a general sense, it is unavoidable that reference to the experience with NOVELL will be found throughout the work.

2
Library Environment

Libraries, regardless of their type, remain service-oriented organizations committed to bringing individuals and information together. Although libraries have been involved in automation of one type or another for years, they continue to be labor intensive organizations. At least part of the reason for this situation is the fact that libraries are, in a significant way, office environments focusing on production activities.

The past decade has witnessed the inception and growth of a mindset among the public and within both private and public institutions that focuses on how increasingly limited resources can be leveraged to improve the effectiveness and productivity of organizations. This has proven, and will continue, to be a major challenge as the range of service expectations held by the public continues to grow and diversify. The result has been a constant search for ways and means to modify and improve the services offered to a clientele while minimizing and/or containing costs. Libraries have been full participants in this activity.

As with mainframe computing in the past, local area networking has been seized upon as a technology that offers a possible solution. A number of reasons have been identified for considering local area networks in an organization. Some of these are as follows:

- sharing of costly peripheral equipment
- sharing of files and programs among users on the network
- communicating among network users using electronic mail
- integrating information processing activities through the distributed processing possible in a network
- eliminating the repetitive handling of data
- facilitating access to highly specialized programs
- improving the storage, retrieval, processing, and distribution of data/information
- providing an acceptable level of security on the data that is being transmitted within an organization

A large number of libraries have not been able to justify the cost of acquisition, installation, and operation of the mainframe- or minicomputer-

23

based integrated library systems or specialized subsystems. Local area networking does offer an alternative approach to entering into the arena of library automation. There are any number of acquisitions, serial check-in, circulation/reserve, and reference systems that operate in the personal computer environment. Local area networking is an attractive avenue for enhancing the power of these modules in a relatively inexpensive manner. This is particularly the case if the library has already begun to use personal computers in its activities.

The impetus to control costs may be the most immediate focus when a local area network is being considered. Although many libraries are part of public organizations that do not have a "bottom line" profit to be concerned about; there is, nevertheless, increasing attention directed to the costs of library operations which cannot be disregarded. A significant cost of library operations can be compared to the cost of office operations of a large business. "Office expenses comprise approximately 25 percent of a company's cost of doing business, and, as the trend toward white-collar employees continues, it is expected that by the end of the decade, office expenses will account for approximately 45 percent of the cost of doing business in a typical company."[1]. Reducing the costs of labor-intensive library activities, redesigning support services, and improving organizational performance provide significant reasons for local area networking.

Most individuals who have spent any time at all in an organization have experienced some attempt at planning. Long-range planning and strategic planning are two types that have enjoyed popularity among organizations. All too often, the average individual develops considerable skepticism about the payoff from the time and energy invested in these planning exercises. Too often the finished products, if they are completed, are filed in a desk drawer and forgotten in the press of trying to keep the organization afloat during a time of crisis.

If local area networking is going to be successful and the investment in equipment, software, and time recouped, then organizational planning is a must. There must be a clear statement of library mission, goals, and objectives, and these in turn must be linked with the library's budget. Unless that is done, effort and energy will be wasted, and demands will be made on the library staff and budget that diminish the library's ability to provide its traditional services. If anyone still believes that automation will save an organization large amounts of money and make life simpler, local area networking will demonstrate otherwise.

If there is a plan for the library's future, long-range, strategic, or otherwise, or if the planning effort is beginning anew, be prepared to build an extensive understanding of three areas. First, an understanding of the technology involved in local area networking needs to be acquired. It is not necessary to become an expert but there should be a comfort level with the terminology and the principles involved. Second, an understanding of the software aspects of local area networks and the differences between networkable software applications and those that work on single, stand-alone personal computers should be achieved. Third, and this may be the most challenging, individuals should expand their knowledge of how the library is organized and the manner in which it completes its work and delivers its services. Each of these areas will be examined briefly.

Understanding the Technology

Acquiring an understanding of the technology can be achieved through several activities. First, begin to read widely in the publications that cover the industry. Journals such as *Byte, Information Management, InfoWorld, PC Week, MacWeek*, and others should be reviewed regularly. Unfortunately, there is not much coverage of local area networking as it relates to libraries except for an occasional article in *Information Technologies and Libraries, Computers in Libraries, Library Hi-Tech, Library Hi-Tech News*, and *Library Computer Systems and Equipment Review*, so an individual should be prepared to examine the literature of related fields such as office automation. Simply remaining current in the field of local area networking will be a demanding task. So much is being written about local area networking and technological change continues to be a hallmark of the field that it is fruitless to assume all the relevant information can be reviewed.

Second, get acquainted with the local computer stores and distributors. In this process, determine which of the firms demonstrate they have the needed levels of network experience. All too often, today, the management of computer stores focus their staff's energies on selling rather than remaining current with the constantly evolving networking technology. When it comes time to install a local area network, knowing knowledgeable individuals can make the task simpler. Talking with these people allows one the opportunity to gain a good sense of what is happening in the marketplace and to find out what salespeople perceive the strengths and weaknesses of the competing systems to be. They may have sample installations that can be explored to build an understanding of how the technology functions.

Network Software

Becoming acquainted with networkable software requires many of the same steps involved in understanding the technology. A major difference is the fact that using some of the software may be necessary. This is not too difficult since many software manufacturers and distributors are willing to provide demonstration disks. Talk to people who are already using networkable software. Find out their assessment, the strengths and weaknesses they have observed from actually installing and operating the software.

Understanding the Library and How It Functions

Third, as important as understanding the technology and comprehending networkable software may be, the most important knowledge to acquire is how the library really functions. It is absolutely essential that the technical, administrative, and human aspects of the libary be investigated and understood. The reason for this stems from the fact that the effective use of a local area network will depend upon the human element. There is an unfortunate tendency to become enamored of the technology allowing it to lead people. If local area networking in libraries is going to be successful, each staff member must help to ensure that people will lead the technology. For this to happen, librarians must have a clear understanding not only of the library's goals but of its culture and working style as well.

There will be a number of issues related to network operation that must be resolved within the context of the existing organization. Such issues include access to the network and user support. You must know who the network users are going to be, the functions to be done at each workstation, and the range of applications that will be needed. As the way in which work is currently done is identified, consideration will have to be given to how it will change in a networked environment. How does information move or flow in the library now and how will that change after a network is installed? What are the relationships that exist between library employees and how will those relationships be altered?

Examine the library's organizational structure and its management hierarchy. It is entirely possible that a fully implemented local area network could permit changes. The presence of a network may change the formal and informal power structures within the library. While there is the expectation that networking will improve productivity, it is also very likely that interpersonal conflict and stress among the staff will increase, at least temporarily, unless steps are taken from the beginning to mitigate that possibility. The fact that some people will have to learn new skills such as keyboarding (probably more of an adjustment for the administrators than anyone else), and nearly everyone will have to get used to a new approach to communication, will make the adaptation to networking an organizational challenge. The possibility of alterations in the relationships between professional and non-professional staff is very real, and considerable thought should be given to how it will be addressed.

Individuals, in libraries or elsewhere, who are already heavily involved in personal computing may assume that they can continue to operate as they have in the past. This, unfortunately, will not be the case. Local area networking creates an environment in which all the members become much more dependent upon one another, particularly for the effective operation of the network. Unlike the individual personal computer, what a person does with a networked workstation, such as moving it, will affect everyone else on the network.

While there is justification for skepticism about the claims surrounding the effect of local area networking on an organization, it does seem clear that the effect can be dramatically positive. "Some studies suggest that an office worker's productivity may be increased twofold through the use of increased automation and local communications capabilities. While one might question such a large estimate, it is generally recognized by most people working in the industry that the local area network does assist in increasing efficiency and productivity within the office."[2]   The real challenge to library administrators is to recognize the opportunities that local area networking technology offers to discover new ways of doing work. What has to be avoided is the situation in which there are "...managers who are trying to do the same old job in the same old way, using 18th-century methods with 20th century tools and ignoring the potential of a system they have already paid for..."[3]

The outcome of the investigation and assessment of the library, the acquisition of an understanding of local area networking technology, and the availability of networkable software should be a decision about whether local area networking is a project the library should undertake. It must be kept in mind that for many small libraries, even if local area networking may be justified, there will not be staff with the needed skills, abilities, or time to devote to the project. If that is the case, then the trade-offs involved in using consultants or other outside specialists will have to be examined.

If a decision is made to select, acquire, install, implement, and then operate a local area network, the easy part of the undertaking is complete. Each of the steps listed in the preceding sentence will be the basis for a chapter that follows. While the chapter structure presents material in a segmented manner, the reality of these phases is that they are integrated and it is often difficult to distinguish between them. The reality of networking is that many activities such as planning and training iterate many times during a local area networking project.

3
LAN Selection

The selection phase may be the most critical of the entire process of moving from a decision that a local area network would be useful to having a local area network operational in a library. A library's decisions or lack of decision-making during this phase will directly influence the prospects for the successful use of the local area network. Rather than one distinct set of activities, there are three separate but highly related activities that must occur: the selection of a local area network administrator; the design of the local area network; and the selection process resulting in the identification of a local area network to be installed and implemented.

In selecting a system that is potentially as critical to the long-term success of an organization as it is technologically complicated, the most important first step is to determine how the library will manage it. If the library is large enough to have established a systems unit, then some of the decisions may have been resolved. If the library has not taken this step then there will be some preliminary adjustments, and for the sake of this chapter, the assumption is made that the library does not have a systems unit.

LAN Administrator

One of the preconditions that needs to be accepted as soon as the decision is made to move into a local area network environment is the necessity of designating someone to be responsible for the network. If the installation, implementation, and use of a local area network is to be successful, this designation must be more than nominal. There are two problems that a library administration will face immediately. First, the inadequate staffing levels in most libraries will force the administration to decide whether this assignment will be a full-time one or if it can be a part-time responsibility. Under no circumstance should it be considered a temporary assignment. In practical terms, even a part-time assignment is probably unrealistic because as the local area network grows, the demands on the network administrator will increase. The second problem relates to where in the organizational hierarchy the network administrator should be placed. A number of reporting relationships can be suggested but in the last analysis the arrangement will depend upon the organizational culture and structure of the library.

The simplest explanation of a local area network administrator's job is that he or she manages the local area network. This individual must have the day-to-day responsibility for the operation of the local area network. This person must have the responsibility, too, for anticipating the growth of the network and planning its expansion. The range of activities for which the network manager will be responsible includes the following functions or disciplines:[1]

- operations
- administration
- maintenance
- configuration management
- documentation/training
- database management
- planning
- security

If a library has a systems or library automation department, this may be the most appropriate place to search for the local area network administrator. It may be that no one within that unit is suitably equipped to carry out the functions of this assignment.

If the library does not have a systems or automation unit, other members of the staff should be considered if they have the needed qualifications or potential. Although the individual characteristics of the LAN administrator will vary from library to library, there are certain qualities that should be present.

Personal Qualities

First, and foremost, this person has to be a people person. The success or failure of network implementation seldom is due to the technical or mechanical aspects of the system. All too often it is due to the inability to communicate with the prospective users of the network to ensure that they understand the limitations of the network. Because network users will bring widely varying levels of expertise and understanding to their use of the network, it is critical that the administrator have the capacity to relate to those staff members who may be computer illiterates as well as to the sophisticates. Tolerance and empathy are important personal characteristics for the administrator. The administrator should expect to spend a substantial part of his or her day out with the staff exploring and listening to how they are using the network, the problems they are having with it, and the other functions they would like to have it assist them in doing.

Second, there is debate about whether the administrator should bring substantial local area networking experience to the position. Is it more important that the individual be knowledgeable about the type of organization involved in the move to local area networking or be an expert in the operation of local area networking? The realities of the marketplace answer some of this concern. It is still true that "experts" in local area networking are relatively scarce and sought out by organizations prepared to pay very competitively for their skills. Regardless of this fact, it is more important for the local area network administrator to be knowledgeable about the type of organization, libraries in this case. The technical skills can be acquired through the training that is usually available from the network vendor. Library administrators should be aware, however, that the more skilled their network administrator becomes, the greater the likelihood the individual may be lured away from the library by salary offers the library administration cannot match.

Third, the administrator should have the capacity to absorb disparate bits of information in a sponge-like manner and then recast them in a way that permits looking at the organization and its work in ways the network can support. At the same time, the administrator must have the ability to make the best use of every scrap of time that becomes available. Even after the local area network is installed, stabilized, and operating regularly, there will be a constant stream of emergencies, problems, and questions from throughout the organization that require immediate reaction. This situation is only accentuated as the organization becomes more dependent on the network. The successful administrator will finally develop a sixth sense about the manner in which the network is functioning and, often, be able to anticipate problems before they become disabling to the network.

Policies and Procedures

Once an individual has been identified to be the local area network administrator and convinced of the wisdom of assuming that task, there are a number of policies and procedures that have to be established in the library. These are indispensable to the success of the local area network administrator but are the responsibility of the library administration to put in place.

The most important is that there will be one and only one person responsible for the administration and/or management of the local area network. This is not an assignment for a committee. *It will not work if a committee tries to manage the network.* One person finally has to be charged with the duty of installing, implementing, and operating the network. Any other approach will compromise the long-term effectiveness of the network and its contribution to the organization. Implied in this charge is a commitment on the part of the library director/administration to support fully the work and recommendations of the local area network administrator.

It is entirely appropriate for library administration to establish a committee to address the broad issues of network administration policy. This body can have representatives from throughout the library and the local area network administrator among it membership. Its task is to establish policy; it is the administrator's assignment to execute the policies.

Library administration should also address the question of whether the local area network administrator will be a "dedicated" or "designated" assignment. The "dedicated" administrator has an assignment that focuses completely on the operation of the network. The "designated" administrator has assumed responsibility for the local area network administration in addition to an existing set of responsibilities. The realities of a library's personnel roster and budget may dictate the answer to this choice. While the initial decision may be dictated, the library administration should be prepared to accommodate the fact that the "designated" administrator will inevitably be transformed into a "dedicated" administrator. The challenges of installation, implementation, maintenance, training, and just listening quickly consume all of an individual's available time.

As the use, extensiveness, and pervasiveness of the local area network develops, it is entirely appropriate that the network administrator begins to develop a corps of assistants scattered throughout the library. These individuals may relate to the administrator in an entirely informal way outside the official structure of the library. They may be formed into an operational committee to provide certain types of support to the administrator. These persons can become specialists in certain aspects of the network such as the use of E-mail, communications (modems), printers, telefacsimile, and such. Ultimately, depending upon the size and complexity of the library, it may be entirely appropriate for local area network supervisors or assistants to be added to the formal organizational structure to assist the network administrator.

An issue that has not yet been addressed is the question of where the local area network administrator should be placed in the organization. It is plausible that the person should be part of a systems unit; it is just as possible for the individual to report directly to the library director. The organizational culture and its readiness to integrate local area networking will influence the resolution of this question.

A final comment regarding the network administrator relates to training-- the administrator's own training and training within the organization. Do not expect the administrator to come to the job with a complete understanding of local area networking in the abstract, or the specific network in question. Local area networking is changing and evolving too quickly for anyone to ever claim they know it all. At best, they can admit they are "survivors" continuing to learn at every opportunity. Training for the administrator and the rest of the library staff who use the local area network is a never ending experience. Successful training simply ensures the ultimate success of the network in helping to modify the way in which work is done in the library, and makes the work more efficient and effective.

The preceding pages should have identified some of the aspects of the position that need to be reflected in the job description for the local area network administrator, as well as some of the abilities that should be sought. "The network manager's administrative abilities should encompass record-keeping, inventory tracking, technical, diagnostic, interpersonal and analytical abilities. Little can overcome weak administrative control of resources..."[2] A concise list of management skills that should be present in a local area network administrator follows:[3]

- administrative control
- record-keeping skills
- inventory-tracking skills
- technical management skills
- ability to make decisions
- ability to establish priorities
- means to cope with staff shortages and burnout
- ability to provide recognition
- skills to develop employees
- team building skills
- evaluation skills

Do not delay identifying and hiring or transferring this individual. The success of the subsequent steps in moving to local area networking will depend on the library administration's commitment to finding the best person to be the local area network administrator.

Designing the LAN

The first task the local area network administrator will undertake is the design of the local area network for the library. This step is a prerequisite to the actual selection process that will identify the brand of network and network vendor the library will use. The design of the local area network will require an extensive assessment of the library and the work it is doing.

The design of the network provides a set of guidelines for preparing the RFP, RFQ, or similar document used to seek possible networking software and hardware that will meet the library's identified needs. It is possible that the design of the local area network is analogous to the building program for a new library or the description of an integrated library system. Each requires an extensive understanding of the existing library and/or its automation capabilities and depends upon an explicit projection of what will be needed for future physical facilities, automation needs, or projected networking hardware and software growth.

There are a handful of very broad-based issues that must be re-examined as part of the local area network design consideration. Whether these are investigated in a formal or informal manner, library administration should record the answers for future reference. There may come a time when library staff will ask why the decision was made to embark on this project or why it was thought to be practical. First, an assessment should be made of whether or not a local area network can be installed in the library. A preliminary answer to this question should have been reached before you proceeded to hire/designate a local area network administrator. Now is the time to eliminate all doubt on this issue. Careful consideration should have been given to whether the benefits from the local area network will outweigh its costs. Consideration should be given to whether, or how much of, the technology already in use within the library or its parent organization can be used to implement the local area network.

The question of benefits versus costs/liabilities may be difficult to answer if the library and/or its parent organization has little experience with personal computing. Some of the potential benefits and pitfalls of local area networks are given here.[4]

Benefits:

- System evolution: incremental changes with contained impact.
- Reliability/availability/survivability: multiple interconnected systems disperse functions.
- Resource sharing: expensive peripherals, hosts, data.
- Multi-vendor support: customer not locked into a single vendor.
- Improved response/performance.
- User needs single terminal to access multiple systems.
- Flexibility of equipment location.
- Integration of data processing and office automation.

Potential Pitfalls:

- Interoperability is not guaranteed: software, data.
- A distributed database raises problems of integrity, security/privacy.
- Creeping escalation: more equipment will be procured than is actually needed.
- Loss of control: more difficult to manage and enforce standards.

Following are some factors to be considered or questions to be asked in local area network design:

What is the purpose of the network? If the purpose of the network is not understood, it will be very difficult to make an accurate assessment of the functions that are needed. Without a clear statement of the network functions there is no foundation for developing the network. The description of the purpose must be as precise as possible. Success in clarifying the purpose will be directly dependent upon involving all the potential users of the projected network.

Projected traffic volume. During the design and selection phase this may be a very difficult task for library personnel, but a projection must be made. This may be one of the situations when the library will have to employ a consultant or computer vendor to develop the forecast. Traffic is the amount of actual data movement over the network cabling. The various applications that will be functioning on the network will influence the traffic load, but each function will wield a different effect on the total network traffic. While this projection is only an estimation, be certain the calculation is on the high side. This will help ensure the network response time remains acceptable.

What will the composition of the network traffic be? This question is related to the previous one. The sources of the network traffic need to be identified. The software applications will influence this but so will traffic factors such as the demand for remote printing, plotters, the use of modems, and facsimile equipment. Software applications that involve a lot of disk accesses, such as database programs, will have a significant impact.

What is the peak traffic volume likely to be? Answering this question requires that the maximum number of users be estimated. A significant factor here will be the number of "high demand" users, individuals who are doing large amounts of I/O, using pagemaking applications, for instance. If an analysis reveals that there may be a half-dozen major users on the network, consideration should be given to providing them with their own local area network. This will enable the major users to work efficienctly at the same time that the majority of the network users have a clean line to use.

Size of the network. This is based on the number of servers, workstations, and peripherals that will be attached to the network. These need to be calculated during the design phase so an accurate network plan can be produced.

Network topology. As mentioned in Chapter 1, this will be influenced by the building in which the network is to be located, the network speed needed, the funds available, and the types of network users. A fact that is often overlooked is that a local area network may have many sub-local area networks. A local area network is determined by the cable from the server, and each independent cable is a separate local area network.

How many network users will there be? In part, this is determined by the number of workstations. It is possible that a library would have a limited number of workstations but still have all library staff trained and expected to use the local area network for appropriate activities. If that is the case, each staff member will have to have a secure personalized part of the network environment established for their use. This is usually done by preparing a separate script for each staff member identifying their network rights.

What is the network user work load likely to be? This will be determined, to a large extent, by the software applications that are loaded on the network. It is conceivable that some library staff members might have only an occasional need to use the network, while others might require almost continuous access. This will have a direct bearing on the number of workstations and peripherals. It may have considerable impact on the training schedules that have to be provided.

What will be the cost of installing and operating the network and training the staff? The answer to this question is dependent upon answering all of the other questions in this chapter. The state of the marketplace, particularly the degree of competitiveness in the local community, may determine the final cost incurred.

What level of security is needed for the network? This is one of the most important issues in local area networking. There are many potential network users who are reluctant to use a local area network because they are afraid others will be able to read their information or destroy their work. Trust and confidence in the capacity of the local area network to protect the individual's work is crucial. Using NOVELL Netware, as an example, a combination of passwords and rights can be used to establish a secure network. If this is done correctly, library staff will acquire the necessary trust in the network over time.

What level of reliability, maintainability, or serviceability is needed for the network? Reliability is like security; network users have to develop confidence that the system will be there when they need to use it. Those network users who have been effective standalone PC users will be reluctant to become completely dependent upon the local area network. To ensure reliability, maintenance should be done during hours the network is not operating or when the library staff has been given sufficient warning the network will be down. An adequate supply of replacement parts will facilitate solving problems when they do arise, and it is certain problems will arise. If service is needed, how much should be expected from properly trained library personnel and how much should come from the network vendor or third-party vendors? Regardless of who provides the service, timeliness of response is the critical issue.

What level of resource sharing is projected? There are two aspects to this question. Software savings can be effected by purchasing site licenses rather than individual copies of the application. Hardware costs can be minimized by purchasing fewer pieces of equipment and placing them conveniently for access and use by natural workgroups.

Accessibility of unique resources. An underlying reason for engaging in any type of networking is access to resources that would not otherwise be available. As a local area network is planned and designed, an assessment of unique local resources should be conducted to determine if there are databases that should be built to make these resources accessible in a networked environment.

How will diagnostics be handled? Network diagnostics need to become a routine part of network operations. If there is continual monitoring of network performance then problems can often be anticipated and corrected before network failure occurs. When network failure does take place, library staff should be trained and equipped to perform at least a minimal level of diagnostics on the network so the causes of problems can be quickly identified.

What hardware specifications are required? This question focuses on the PCs and terminals that will be needed for network use. As a network is installed, there will be an existing base of computing equipment that will have to be connected to the local area network. This may require a substantial effort on the part of the network administrator. The variety of computing equipment available for sale and the range of computing skills that library staff will bring to the network will force a constant balancing act between available equipment, staff desires, and budget limitations.

What level of documentation is required to describe the local area network? Most organizations that begin local area networking put off the creation of network documentation until after the first crisis or catastrophe occurs. From the day the first discussions about the possibility of local area networking taking place in a library occur, a documented record of every action, decision, and discussion should be made. It may be possible to have too much documentation, but it is hard to imagine that situation. Human nature seems to rebel against adequate documentation being produced. If there is sufficient library staff, the task of preparing documentation and maintaining a paper trail on network decisions should be assigned to one staff member.

What evaluation standards and documentation will be needed to monitor the local area network? This will vary among networks. As a library becomes increasingly dependent on a local area network functioning with no downtime, more attention has to be devoted to a daily evaluation of network performance. In a situation where an OPAC has been made available over a network to hundreds of patrons at the same time that office applications are extended to library staff, the evaluation process, the performance standards to be met, and the documentation of performance to be maintained take on added importance. There are a variety of hardware and software tools available for performing diagnostics on a network to determine its functionality. These tools will range in price from less than $100 to more than $10,000. The particular approach a library chooses will depend on the assessment of its own needs for regular network performance evaluation and the extent of that evaluation. Regardless of the approach taken or the tools used, remember to document the process and record the results so that there are benchmarks against which future evaluations can be compared.

What physical constraints exist in the library? How old is the library building? Is it part of a campus or municipal or corporate facility? Does the internal wiring comply with existing codes? How thick are the walls? Where are the workspaces and office located? Will workstations be too far apart or too close together? These and hundreds of other physical factors characterizing the structure housing the library will influence what may or may not be able to be done with local area networking.

What budgetary constraints exist in the library? Aside from the fact that all libraries have inadequate budgets, what is the budget cycle the library must use? Are there special purchasing requirements that must be followed? Are consultants permitted by the parent organization? Can equipment be lease-purchased or must it all be acquired outright? A clear understanding of the entire budget process will facilitate making the decisions that will be needed to acquire and implement a local area network.

What technology constraints exist in the library? It is possible that some existing computing equipment in a library should be left outside the local area network. The fact that this may delay some library staff having access to the network could cause morale problems unless anticipated during the planning. Does the library have sufficient power, and clean power, to support a local area network with growing traffic demands? Inevitably, unless the library is in a new building, old and new technologies will have to be merged.

What problems exist in the way information moves or work is done in the library? The way in which work is done in a non-networked environment may differ substantially from the possibilities that could be achieved when a local area network is installed. How many redundant steps in the manual processes can be eliminated if library staff can access a networked database?

This list is not exhaustive by any means but it provides an indication of the breadth of the investigation that must occur in the design phase.

Michael Hordeski has identified "six profiles that can be used to define the local network design criteria:

- the user profile
- the usage profile
- the geographic profile
- the applications profile
- the hardware profile
- the special requirements profile

These profiles allow a description of the present and potential local network users and their environment. Most profiles should be prepared for several time periods, because some information will remain the same while other factors might be constantly changing."[5]

The first of these profiles is an inventory of each department or unit in the library. Among other information that should be collected is the number of people in each unit in the library, what each of the individuals do, job descriptions and titles, and the configuration of formal and informal workgroups. The usage profile examines the programs and software packages in use, whether access to external resources is needed, the peak activity periods, and types of data being processed. As these data are gathered there should be some attempt to assess the probable impact of system failure or network downtime. The geographic profile should provide a map of the distribution of the prospective network users now and at varying times in the future. Reviewing the manner in which automation is already being used in library departments to complete work should provide information for the applications profile. An extensive detailed equipment inventory should supply the data required to assemble the hardware profile. Brands, model numbers, sizes, speeds, and year of the equipment should be included at a minimum. This may be the most revealing part of the local area network design process, for you may already have a larger investment in useful equipment than anticipated. Gathering this array of information will require the use of personal interviews with library staff as well as several surveys of different aspects of the library's operations.

Site Visits

An important step in preparing the local area network design is to be able to view other networks in operation. This is the best way to identify features that might otherwise have been overlooked but could be valuable for the library. Site visits offer the chance to avoid problems that other organizations have experienced. These visits can provide an opportunity to evaluate different brands of networks, observing the respective strengths and weaknesses and assessing the relative costs.

Hardware

It is critical to keep in mind that local area networks require a substantial number of different pieces of equipment in order to be functional, particularly as they begin to grow. Terminals, monitors, multiplexers, transceivers, connectors, switches, modems, and such, must be identified as required pieces and then manufacturer and model possibilities need to be reviewed and chosen.

Maintainability/Serviceability

How easy will it be to install the network that is finally selected? Will library staff or parent organization staff be able to install the network or will it require personnel with special skills and training? Since all networks inevitably seem to grow, how difficult is it to expand the network? How difficult is it to maintain or repair the local area network? Can preventive maintenance be done by in-house staff or will all maintenance, preventive and corrective, have to be performed by outside personnel? The local area network administrator must establish standards that the library considers to be reasonable before the selection process begins.

Although it will be difficult to be patient, the installation and operationalizing of new network software take time. This is particularly true when network software is being upgraded. There is a natural tendency to assume the upgrade is only an expansion of the previous version of the network. While that may be true, it does not mean that significant changes were not made in the software. Go slow and do it right the first time. Even though this may extend the process several days or weeks, library staff attitudes will be positive if the migration is successful the first time.

Reliability

The worst thing that can happen to any automated system, and especially a local area network, is for it to fail. How critical is the functioning of the network to the library? The more important the continuous operation of the network, the greater the cost implications for the library. Possible failure in a local area network can include losing communication with a node on the network, the loss of functionality in the central hub, and power interruptions that cause the entire network to fail. Following are some issues to consider when evaluating vulnerability:[6]

- Does the network have a single central element? If so, is it protected with automatic switching or redundancy?
- Do all signals have to pass through a single element? If so, are provisions made for automatic bypass? If the element is bypassed, are the adjacent nodes still within signaling distance of each other?
- What is the meantime between failure and the meantime to repair the total network?
- Is the technology mature enough that the predicted evidence of failure is accurate, or does it rely on unproven engineering estimates?
- How readily accessible are the vendor's repair forces?

Cost

The cost of local area networking may be overlooked, but it can never be ignored for long. Because the personal computing marketplace is so volatile, trying to establish price comparisons and evaluate all the factors that contribute to the cost of a local area network can be an enormous undertaking, but it is essential. Several distinct areas of cost can be easily identified:

- hardware and connection costs
- installation costs
- communications costs
- software costs
- maintenance costs
- downtime costs
- training costs

The natural tendency is to focus on the first two cost categories--hardware and installation--but they may constitute only a small portion of the cost of acquiring and operating a local area network over the life of the network.

Because the personal computing industry is so competitive, the advice of Rowland Archer is useful: "Follow two rules of thumb: choose a vendor who is actively working with new technology so that expansion of your LAN in the future will benefit from reduced costs, and do not buy more hardware than you need as long as prices continue to fall over time."[7]

Software

The first fact to know is that there will be two separate groups of software in the networked environment. There will be application software similar to that used on standalone PCs. In addition, there will be network control programs, the network operating system. Each of these presents its own unique set of challenges.

Gradually, vendors have moved many software applications from the standalone PC environment to the multi-user network environment. The reluctance to move as quickly as users would have liked was due to the inability to create a clearly effective way to monitor and charge for multiple uses of the software. Two methods have evolved--site licenses and software locks--that permit only a previously licensed number of users to work with the software at one time. Ultimately, most libraries will be using software under both arrangements.

The network operating system software will be loaded on the network file server. Its purpose is to facilitate network access to the rest of the network and give directions to the network. This software coordinates the activities of all of the nodes on the network. Choose this software with great care for it will affect the effectiveness of the library's network. After careful examination and use of other network operating systems, the authors settled upon NOVELL's Netware four years ago for use in their library. Netware has continued to serve as the local area network has migrated from a three-station network to a network of seven LANs, three servers, and sixty local terminals, featuring remote call-in computers installed for outside use, and a bridge to a campus fiber backbone that permits access to BITNET and INTERNET.

Security

Although this topic will be addressed in a later chapter, some review is relevant now. In the design phase, evaluate how critical security of the network's transmissions and data are. If the library is part of an organization that has reason to be concerned about the integrity of its information resources, then security issues should begin with decisions related to the type of wiring to be used for the library's network. If security is not so critical, then it may be possible to satisfy security needs through software protection such as passwords and some rudimentary levels of encryption. Whatever the assessment, this is the time to resolve the issue since installation and implementation of security measures is infinitely easier at the outset.

Environment

There are a variety of questions that should be answered about the physical library site at this stage.

- Where are the nodes located--throughout a building, on only one floor, or in one department?
- How are the workstations distributed--are they concentrated in a very restricted area?
- Where will the cabling be installed--the ceiling, ducts, underground?
- What distances will the cabling have to be pulled?
- Where can the central networking equipment be placed to enable maintenance and repair to take place easily?

If the local area network is to be installed in an older building, then existing conditions may limit or even preclude certain network options. Installing a network in a new building can be relatively simple if the architects and organization planners have been convinced that installing electronics, communications, and network technologies during construction is cost-effective.

Before preparing the bid documents for distribution to prospective vendors, it may be appropriate to review what should have been done by this time and what remains to be accomplished. First, there should be a succinct definition of what the local area network is to do. Second, a variety of data should have been collected regarding the requirements for the network being planned. At a minimum these requirements would include: information transfer needs, the network topology needed for the building, possible linkages, potential growth requirements, planned or initial linkages to other networks. Third, the site plan for the facility should have been completed.

The Selection Process

The completion of the local area network design should lead naturally into the preparation of the RFP, RFQ, or other bid documents that must be produced before the local area network components can be selected in marketplace. If there is no requirement to use a bid procedure, there is still substantial value to be gained from creating a description of both the requirements and the acceptable levels of performance that must be demonstrated before a vendor will be considered.

Many of the approaches taken in acquiring an integrated library system can be transferred to the local area network selection process. One of the most important mechanisms to adapt or create is the matrix of qualities that are considered important to a local area network for the library and the weights that each quality will bring to the final decision. All of this should be settled and written down at the time the design is completed.

A number of factors may be assigned varying degrees of importance in the process of selecting the local area network. Their importance will depend upon the library's unique set of circumstances and its membership in a larger organization. These are not listed in any particular order.

- Compliance with existing national and international standards.
- Is the local area network supported by major hardware and software vendors?
- Are future cost reduction opportunities apparent?
- Is there a variety of software applications available for the network?
- What transmission techniques are used?
- Are either voice or video applications supported?
- Availability of required hardware and software.
- Pricing.
- The manner in which workstations are connected to the network.
- Topology.
- Ease of installation.
- Security options.
- Flexibility and expandability.
- Number of different functions that are supported.
- Error rates on network.
- How available is the network to a user?
- Length of time it takes for a message to transit the network.
- Throughput, data transmission rate.
- Connectivity options to other networks inside the library, outside the library yet within the larger organization, and to distant networks.
- Availability of training programs from vendor.
- System reliability.
- Availability of service and maintenance.
- Stability and fiscal viability of the vendor.

In the final analysis, library staff charged with the responsibility of selecting the local area network must be convinced that the particular product has the capacity "to solve a problem; enhance the library's operation; and increase user productivity."[8]

While all of the factors listed above could be made part of the decision matrix used to evaluate prospective networks, in reality there are too many. Experience has demonstrated that approximately ten criteria provide a more workable list. The criteria that are selected can be weighted to reflect their relative importance in determining the successful network.

> System Availability and Reliability is considered one of the more important criterion and includes hardware, software, and operational performance. Functional requirements for Response Time and for Growth Capability must be met by all proposed candidates, although individual response rates as well as capacity for growth may vary from candidate to candidate. Training Requirements and Ease of Operation are expected to be minimal for all candidates and ideally should be transparent to the user. Compatibility and Connectivity will vary with each proposed candidate, with some exhibiting more flexibility than others. Maintenance and Logistics Support would affect reliability, but is considered to be a separate characteristic.
> All proposed candidates must meet the minimum functional Security requirements, although some candidates may provide a greater capability in this area. Transition Impact will vary between the proposed candidates, but can be minimized with proper management and scheduling....[9]

The evaluation of the network software and hardware, its ease of installation, and who will do the installation, are important decisions that will have to be made. It is quite possible that a library may have adequately trained staff in the library or the larger organization who can carry out the installation. It is possible that even if the library does have adequately trained staff, it may be appropriate to have them trained so they can perform the work. If it is decided that the library will rely on outside vendor installation there are several things that should be considered. Will the installer work on equipment that is already in the library that is to be part of the network and will they work on network equipment that is not purchased from them. Is the installation cost part of the network price or is it a separate charge?

The vendors finally selected may have more influence on the success or failure of the network hardware and software than the quality of these items. All other characteristics and features of the network being equal, the vendors must finally tip the direction of the library's decision. This is where conversation with other organizations that have already been involved with local area networking can be invaluable. Librarians have well-established networks within the profession that can facilitate the sharing of experiences and information and they should be used. Do not be afraid to ask others for their opinions.

While some service and support from a vendor should be part of the initial purchase of a network, there is a limit to what can be expected from a vendor without additional charge. The support needed from a vendor may be extensive if there are serious problems with the network and it is unreasonable to think there will not be a charge. The vendor must cover its costs to remain in business, and service and support are two large cost centers that must generate revenue.

Questions that should be asked of a prospective vendor include the following:[10]

- How available is the repair force?
- What kind of support does the vendor offer in keeping the network upgraded with enhancements? What is the average for upgrades?
- Is the vendor likely to join the list of failing data equipment manufacturers?
- What kind of warranty service does the vendor offer?
- What kind of technical assistance is available? Is it available on a 24-hour basis, or only eight hours per day--perhaps only five hours per day if the vendor is on the opposite end of the continent? (It is expensive to equip and maintain a user support force. Minimizing user support is one way some vendors offer a product for a lower price than their competitors.)
- What is the vendor's reputation among users for supporting a product once it is sold?
- Does the vendor offer full support features such as engineering and installation of the network?

As mentioned previously, other local area network users can provide the best assessment of the type of service and support that can be anticipated from a vendor. Vendors should provide a list of references without being asked. One aspect of vendor performance that should be of particular interest is how well they have met the timetables they have established. As part of the proposal that a vendor submits, there should be an installation and implementation timetable. If there is one place where Murphy's Laws may work, it is the timetable; so try to determine if the vendor has provided for unexpected problems and has identified contingencies for addressing changed circumstances that will ensure the local area network becoming operational as forecast.

When the review of competing vendors and products is complete, the selection of the local area network software, the topology, the hardware, and the cabling media should be settled expeditiously. With those decisions complete, the next step is to plan the installation and implementation. This will include reviewing and refining initial installation plans, ordering the local area network software and hardware, and requesting necessary modifications to the library.

4
LAN Installation

The installation phase of local area networking is the logical extension of the process of selecting local area network software, hardware, and possibly a vendor. The success or failure, or perhaps, the lack of pain, of this phase is a direct consequence of the quality of preparation that occurs in the selection phase. If shortcuts are taken, steps omitted, and decisions are not based on the facts of the analysis the results will be evident as the installation of the local area network takes place.

As important as the network administrator may be to moving the library and its staff through the selection process, the real test of that individual's fortitude will occur during installation. During installation phase there will be many opportunities to discover just how effective the local area network administrator's interpersonal skills are, how deep the commitment to detail is, and the level of perseverance the person has in the face of seemingly overwhelming obstacles. It is sufficient to say that in spite of meticulous preparations, Murphy's Law will be demonstrated time and again during installation. This will be true regardless of the size of the library or the complexity of the local area network being installed.

It is too easy to be caught up in the rush to install the network and, in the process, forget some very practical considerations that will help make the installation process simpler. Perhaps the overriding rule should be: assemble the local area network by installing it in building blocks. Begin with the simplest, most elementary pieces of the network based on the design. Assemble these few pieces. Test them, being certain to determine they work as planned. Once it has been confirmed they work as planned, add on the next logical section and repeat the testing. In this manner, as each additional part or feature of the network is added, it is layered onto a network that has been tested and found acceptable.

As the installation process is anticipated, there will probably be three choices: First, if the network software and hardware have been acquired from a single vendor, that organization may include installation as an optional part of the bid or purchase price. Second, if a consultant has been used to assist in the design and selection phases, that individual or company may have included installation either as part of its contract or as an add-on cost. Third, it may be decided, regardless of how the equipment and software has been acquired or whether a consultant has been used, to have library staff undertake installation. The reasonableness of this approach will depend, obviously, on whether the library has qualified staff to take on the project or whether the larger institution or organization requires that the library use its personnel for such tasks.

There are some questions that should be asked about the installation process that may help in making the decision about who will do the work.[1]

- What skill levels are needed to install and test the network? Are these skills readily available on the labor market?
- Are specialized tools and test equipment needed? Can they be rented? Will the vendor supply them?
- What is your cost estimate for installation? How does it compare to the vendor's installation price?
- Are the installation and testing instructions well-documented?
- Does your locality require a license for cable installation?
- What building or fire codes may restrict the type of cabling? Will special jacketing such as Teflon or conduit be required?

Role of the Network Administrator

Rather than review the installation steps at this time, it is more appropriate to examine the role of the local area network administrator in the installation phase. Although it has been stated earlier in the book, it is time to repeat: the administration of a local area network including its installation is not a task for a committee. The local area network administrator has been hired to oversee, direct, and manage the installation of the network. It may be appropriate to have a committee that addresses long-range strategic issues, policy planning, and fiscal issues, but it should not meddle in the day-to-day installation activities.

The network administrator should have planned the installation process so that there is a set of identifiable and known milestones that can be used to measure progress during the installation. The administrator should have established a training or staff development schedule for the entire library staff that will not only introduce them to the concept of local area networking, but provide them with the necessary level of training to allow them to begin making use of the network. In the process of establishing the training schedule and conducting the training, the network administrator should be focusing on two organizational goals. The first of these is to reduce or minimize the uncertainty surrounding the installation of the network. Anytime there are changes in the workplace and work routines, there will be considerable ambivalence in the way in which staff members view their work. An orderly, well-planned installation that keeps the staff informed will minimize much of the uncertainty. At the same time, the network administrator should be a moving force in the review of existing job descriptions and the development of revised performance standards for individual staff members and workgroups in the context of the new network. The subject of network training for library staff will be covered later in this chapter.

Returning to a point made earlier, library administration should publicly announce to the staff and any other constituencies that are involved in the networking project that the network administrator is to be the single point of contact with the company or companies from which the network is being acquired. If the installation has been contracted out, the administrator should be the single contact point for that, as well. This should minimize confusion in seeking individuals who have the authority and the responsibility for making the many decisions that will inevitably have to be resolved as the installation proceeds.

Whether another staff member is officially designated the assistant local area network administrator, assigned that task temporarily, or given the task informally, a back-up network administrator is needed. After all, there are only so many hours that an individual can work before he/she collapses or burns out. The assistant is organizational insurance for the long-term usefulness of the network administrator.

As the network administrator begins to work through the steps in the installation process, he or she must remember: *as each action is taken in the installation, document what is done, how it is done, and what is used in terms of tools and equipment.* Unless there is a record detailing how the network was installed and why certain actions were taken, when problems arise later there will be no guide to locate where they are occuring and how they can be corrected. The need for this will be presented again, later in the chapter.

The Installation Process

There are a variety of steps that should be considered as parts of the installation process. Whether a particular step has application to the local situation will depend upon an assessment of local circumstances. While the following list is couched in terms of Ethernet installation, the list has broader application to any type of network.[2]

- preparation of the site
- cable testing and installation
- preparation of the cable for installation of taps and transceivers
- installation of taps and transceivers

- installation of bulkhead wire assemblies on host processors
- host processor preparation for installation of network controller
- installation of network controller
- diagnostic checkout of installed components
- adjustment of system parameters for communications hardware and software
- installation of communications software
- configuration of the network database
- activation of the network software
- testing of network software/hardware
- throughput analysis
- user training
- turnover for use

Site Preparation

The extent of the site preparation required will be dictated by the nature of the site. If the network is being installed in a new library building, many items related to site preparation simply will not occur if the networked environment has been specified as part of the building program. The more common and challenging situation most librarians face is that of trying to install a network in a facility that was constructed with nothing like a network in mind.

Although a general wiring diagram may have been prepared as part of the design and selection phase, there will be a need to move to a deeper level of specificity in dealing with the existing building. The first thing to be done is to obtain the most current blueprints, floorplans, and diagrams of the building. It is certain that the arrangement of offices, work areas, stack areas, and public service locations will have changed over time. Before beginning to write the work orders for changes to be made by electricians, carpenters, or others, walk through the building with the layouts. Look at each of the spaces, making notes to describe any changes that are not recorded. Taking the time to do this can save a substantial amount of wasted effort and money.

This is the time to check the local building, fire, and electrical codes regarding the installation of network cabling. It is possible that specially trained electricians who have been licensed to do the work will have to be used, rather than library staff. This could result in an ugly budgetary surprise.

Cable Testing and Installation

There is a natural tendency to wait until after the cable has been pulled and hardware connected to test the wiring. Do not wait. Test the cable while it is still in a roll. This can be done with an Ohmmeter or, if one is accessible or the purchase can be justified, a Time Domain Reflectometer. Either of these instruments will indicate whether there are breaks or impediments in the cable that might interrupt the transmission of signals.

Long before the installation phase begins, the wiring medium should have been chosen. The several types were reviewed earlier. As preparations for the actual installation proceed, there may still be a temptation to cut corners by using wiring that may already be in the walls. It may have been concluded that there is sufficient surplus twisted pair telephone wiring to support a local area network. Beware of at least two potential problems. First, noise or interference could make a network using twisted pair dysfunctional. Second, the wiring itself could be old, cracked, or broken so that signal transmission is impossible. If a decision has been made to use twisted pair, the library may be better served by installing new wiring.

The ideal environment for cable installation might be a facility in which the wiring could be strung through plenums without any concern for sources of interference, with no need for raceways or trays, and with no codes to meet. In most libraries, the ideal will not exist. Cable distribution will probably use one of the methods detailed below:[3]

- *Surface raceways* are covered metal channels that can be attached to walls and routed wherever necessary. This method of installation is simple, protects the cable, and is easy to maintain and modify. By using surface raceways, you avoid the expense of going inside existing walls, ceiling, or floors.

- *Conduit* is a metal pipe used to shield cable. Many local codes permit conduit-shielded cable to be run on the surface, as with surface raceways or through walls and ceilings.

- *Use of over-ceiling cable trays* is ideal, provided that the over-ceiling space is accessible. Offices with drop ceilings frequently use this method of cable distribution. Cables are brought down to PC level through wall partitions. . . . Over-ceiling routing of non-conduit cable runs is often the most practical and inexpensive solution, particularly in small installations.

Everyone should be aware that the cable coating may cause code compliance problems for a library. PVC cable emits a toxic gas when it burns, and as a result it has been banned from use in return air plenums-- dropped ceilings. The alternative is to route the cable elsewhere or use a more expensive cable coated in Teflon.

If the decision has been made to surface mount network cable in the library, the cable should probably be covered by cable guards. While fiber optic or twisted pair will standup to book trucks rolling over them and being kicked inadvertently by staff, coaxial cable will kink and cease functioning.

Remember, too, that noise or interference in the environment will affect the quality of transmission in the network. This concern should have been investigated during the design phase by identifying the probable sources of interference that are present in the facility to be networked. Electrical motors, especially elevators, fluorescent lights, ballasts, and other wiring that may already be present in the library can be sources of either radio frequency interference (RFI) or electromagnetic interference (EMI).

Another aspect of wiring that is often overlooked until a problem arises is the accessibility of the cabling. Keep in mind that unless library network staff are unbelievably lucky they will have to access the cable many times in the future to repair breaks in the cable, add new equipment, or extend the network. The easier the access, the faster problems can be corrected in the future.

The natural tendency when pulling cable for network installation is to focus on the cable needed for the current configuration. While additional cable is going to be inexpensive, the cost of pulling additional cable in the future could turn out to be a major cost when network expansion is needed. If at all possible, additional cable should be pulled at the time of the initial cable installation. Although it does not qualify as additional cable, remember to leave enough slack in the drop cables that connect to the PCs so they can be moved a reasonable distance from their original location. It is a fact of life that staff will rearrange their offices and workspaces, so be certain there is sufficient cable to accommodate their changes.

In a similar vein, the possibility of pulling fiber optic cable at the time of the first network installation should be given careful consideration. Although fiber optic cable may seem to be more expensive, it provides sufficient bandwidth so the need for rewiring the network can be avoided reducing total life cycle costs. The ready availability of additional bandwidth can facilitate the migration of the network to supporting functions beyond the current data and voice applications.

In addition to these several concerns, be certain that the following kinds of vendor requirements are met as cable is pulled:[4]

- minimum separation between connections to the cable
- maximum lengths of cable runs

- proper termination at the ends of the cable
- use of drop cables from the trunk to a workstation or server
- repeaters to boost the signal over long distances
- routing away from sources of electrical interference such as AC wiring, motors, and fluorescent light fixtures

As the network cable is installed, a floorplan layout of the wiring should be made, preferably to scale. This floorplan will be the road map of the network and should be kept up to date at all times. Instill in all staff involved in the maintenance and operation of the network that no physical changes in the network are made unless they are recorded on the network floorplan. The information on the layout should include the following.

- routing/direction of the cable
- access points to the cable
- all taps on to the network
- all branches in the network
- any splitters that are used
- any connectors that are installed
- terminations that are made in the cable
- amplifiers that are installed
- any headend equipment that is installed

The quality of this record keeping and the level of detail will have a direct effect on the ability of library staff or other maintenance personnel to locate and correct problems in the future.

Documentation

This item is not an explicit step in the installation process. Instead, it is implicit in every part of the installation process and should become second nature to all staff involved in setting up the network. There seems to be a law of nature related to automation, and networking in particular, to the effect that the indispensable piece of information about the installation or configuration is not recorded anywhere. To avoid that problem, make it a practice to record everything. The reasons for the network's configuration, unique problems encountered while installing the wiring, the types of connections used, and the ways in which they have been installed, should all be recorded. Remember that the current local area network administrator may not always be with the library, and someone coming later will be hard-pressed to read the administrator's mind.

An installation log should be created that describes the physical and electronic limits of the network, the number of nodes as well as their locations, the cable runs between workstations, and each piece of hardware used in constructing the network, including brand, model number, and supplier.

The following advice from an article in *LAN Times* has the potential to help novices avoid future frustration:

> Smart administrators and LAN dealers document, within reach of each workstation and file server, unusual switch settings, software configurations, and other out-of-the-ordinary information. Never hide documentation.
>
> Every piece of equipment comes with a registration card. Even though some look more like marketing questionnaires, fill them out and send them in. Proof of purchase date is often not enough to get equipment under warranty serviced quickly.
>
> Without registrations, it's easy to miss important software revisions and product information. It also makes warranty repairs a hassle for all.[5]

Keep track of who, within the library or parent organization or among the vendors, is responsible for maintaining or repairing each piece of equipment that has been acquired. At the same time maintain a repair or maintenance history on each piece of equipment. In addition to all of the previously mentioned documentation, the network administrator will be well-served by maintaining a diary of the things that happen with the network, the bad and the good. This is one of the few ways in which trends may be identified. It can provide the library with verification of the need for network expansion and underscore why one type or brand of equipment is better than another. Equipment records and diaries are one method of minimizing the purchase of incompatible equipment and the use of superseded standards.

Connectors/Terminators

Connectors, terminators, and other small seemingly insignificant pieces of equipment are absolutely essential to the effective functioning of the local area network. In addition to problems related to staff, problems related to these pieces of equipment may cause more headaches than any other part of the network.

Connectors may provide the link between the drop cable and the PC. In a Cheapernet environment the cable can only be connected by a tee; there is no drop cable as there is in a traditional Corvus "twisted pair" configuration. Connectors also attach the drop cable to the main transmission cable in a bus configuration. Several types of connectors are available on the market today. Choose the one that is likely to cause the least amount of trouble. All too often, faulty connectors or poor installation of connectors turns out to be one of the major causes of network failure. No network will operate any better than these links that tie the network together.

While attaching the connector or terminator to a cable is not complicated and does not require sophisticated tools, it does take care and patience to be certain the mating is solid. Using proper tools for network installation can make the process much more rewarding. Often library staff will skimp on equipment to install the network (for example, using pliers to crimp the end of a cable rather than the proper tool). This might work, for a little while or a long time, but the connection is probably not going to be permanent.

One of the often forgotten costs associated with the installation of a network is for the "little" pieces of the network, which are indispensable (e.g. terminators, connectors, fiber optics, etc.). A supply of them should be kept on hand at all times because many of these items can be damaged very easily, which could result in the malfunction of a PC linked to the network. This stockpile should be centrally held, and managed by the network administrator. Only the network administrator, an assistant, or properly trained maintenance or repair personnel should be authorized to work with these items.

Tools

Whether a library decides to hire out its network installation or do its own, it might be wise to create a network briefcase or suitcase. This would contain a variety of documentation and equipment that may be useful in whatever installation approach is utilized and, later, facilitate problem-solving anywhere in the network. The following items should be included in this collection:

- manuals for all the network interface cards used in the network
- several spare network interface cards
- a number of the terminators used on the network
- a number of the connectors, tees, etc., being used
- a copy of a utility software package, such as Norton Utilities
- a spare floppy drive--one of each that the library has in use should be kept on hand
- a good tool kit containing all necessary screw drivers and nut drivers
- a chip puller
- soldering iron and required materials

Whenever a consumable item is used from the network case, replace it immediately, otherwise there will be a network crisis and the needed item won't be there.

If a library has made a commitment to repairing and maintaining its own audiovisual and media equipment, much of the equipment may already be available. This is a network cost that is often overlooked in planning. Depending upon the breadth of the repair and maintenance the library decides to do with its own staff, the cost of acquiring and maintaining the facility can become significant.

If the library has not committed space to house repair/maintenance activities this can be a difficult cost to accommodate in the budget. While an oversized closet could be used, the quality of the work done will be directly affected. A minimum of 150 sq. ft. and probably as much as 400 sq. ft. is needed to provide the type of workspace and storage that will be needed over time. In the best of all worlds, this space should be adjacent to the room in which the network servers, terminals, and other central equipment is located. A repair/maintenance room should be equipped with the following:

- A large table for laying out equipment.
- Sufficient clean power to handle a mini-network.
- Shelf space for all of the reference books and manuals that are accumulated. There may be as many as a dozen manuals with a NOVELL network.
- Table vice for working on small items.
- Good quality, accurate voltage meter.
- Spare cabling for each type in use with the network.
- Adequate lighting.

Network Failures

As soon as a local area network is installed, network failures will occur. No matter how much attention is focused on designing and installing the network to ensure that it is properly configured, failures will happen. Often they are completely outside the ability of anyone to control. For starters, the local utility company's power transmission has many peaks and valleys. A utility crew could accidently cut the main power line into the library; a maintenance crew working in the library could simply switch off a transformer without bothering to check with library personnel, let alone inform them ahead of time so precautions can be taken; these, along with numerous other possibilities, can result in network failure. Perhaps a more frustrating cause is the failure of library personnel to remember that they are now living in a networked environment and their actions can affect the entire library. Before the network was installed, a PC could be moved at any time and placed anywhere a staff member wished. As a participant in a network, it is hard for staff members to remember the drastic consequences of moving a PC without notifying the network administrator. Individual PC autonomy is one of the "freedoms" that is minimized as a library moves into a local area network.

Security

Libraries have always been concerned about security for the collection and patrons, but security as it affects a local area network is another matter entirely. Security for an integrated library system, while a concern, has never seemed to be as troublesome a problem as security for the local area network. One of the reasons for this is that local area networks are made up, by and large, of PCs, and PCs seem to attract a different level of mischief whether it is hackers or individuals intent on obtaining data that is confidential and restricted in its distribution.

Training

Training staff to use a local area network is such a critical part of the process of bringing a network online that it cannot be over-emphasized. Ten questions and/or issues can provide a focus for the discussion of training:

1. What is the need for an in-house trainer; can the library afford not to have one?
2. What role should outside trainers play?
3. What will training cost?
4. What time will be required for training?
5. What capacity does the staff have to learn new skills?
6. Where will the training take place?
7. What is needed, one-time training versus on-going training?
8. Should a training needs analysis be done?
9. What feedback should be obtained from staff about the training of employees?
10. What fears will have to be confronted in order for the training to be successful?

The bottom line is that training is the part of investment that will ensure the success or failure of the rest of the investment in local area networking. Do not scrimp on supporting this phase of networking! Do not forget that *training is an ongoing cost*. The type of training available to library staff will have to be evaluated periodically as they become more effective users of the network.

Local area networking in libraries, or any organization, is filled with a variety of not-too-pleasant realizations for management. Perhaps the most dramatic of these is the reality of hidden and soft costs associated with the implementation and continued use of the local area network. As the installation and implementation of a network is projected, it is possible to identify the cost of equipment, the cost of software, the cost of physical alterations to the environment; it is much more difficult to forecast the probable cost of training the local area network administrator, his/her associates, and the library staff. The easiest approach may be to make a wild guess and then increase that estimate by 50 percent to 100 percent.

The reality of local area network training is that no library can do without it, but it is only as effective as the library administration makes it. The library administration must demonstrate the importance of training by being willing to participate in the process. This is not just good management sense, it is also necessary because the typical library manager initially will be just as unprepared as the rest of the staff to make even minimal use of the network's potential.

It may be appropriate to distinguish at this point between training for the local area network administrator and training for the remainder of the staff. While occasionally there is overlap, these are two very different training needs. The administrator must develop an understanding of the local area network as a complete system knowing how the hardware and software components relate to one another. The staff need to gain an understanding of how to use the features of the network such as electronic mail that will enable them to perform their jobs.

The ten issues listed above, which you should consider as you begin to address the issue of training the LAN administrator and the balance of the staff, will be discussed separately.

Need for an in-house trainer. In the long run, a library must develop a cadre of staff who are able to function as trainers for other staff. This capacity to train staff is needed in a minimal way to ensure that new staff coming to work in the library are provided with a basic set of skills in using the local area network. The reality of most workplaces is that some staff voluntarily will take on the role of trainers for their peers. This may be fine to begin with, but it soon presents a problem since the informal training demands eat away at the time they have available for their primary assignments. It is more effective for libraries to anticipate this situation and work to identify those staff who have the natural skills and an inclination to be trainers, and then modify their job descriptions so the activity is a regular part of their assignment. This will permit jobs to be upgraded so the staff can be compensated properly for the new set of tasks they have assumed. It will also identify those library staff mambers who should receive the often specialized training that vendors sell.

Role of outside trainers. Using outside trainers is probably unavoidable for most organizations, if only to guarantee that the local area network administrator is provided with the opportunity to learn from trained experts. Outside training will be expensive--as much as $1,000 per day plus travel and per diem for the staff member. Typically, there may be a basic training seminar of three or four days that can be followed later with an advanced training program of similar length. By the time the LAN administrator has been through a vendor's complete training program, it is possible that the library will have invested $5,000 in the effort. The payoff is in a smooth and relatively trouble-free implementation. It is unrealistic to believe any implementation will ever be completely trouble-free, but outside or vendor training should minimize the number and frequency of headaches. There is a potential problem that lurks in utilizing outside trainers, however. As they become acquainted with your key network staff, they may attempt to hire them away from the library. If key network staff are lost, the library will have to reabsorb the training costs again, perhaps, hire the trained individual that could not be afforded initially, or accept a decline in the level of network performance because of a lack of network administrator skills.

If outside trainers are used, be certain that they provide the specific training needed by library staff. There is such a diversity of training available in the marketplace today that it is possible to choose the wrong training program or trainers. As in so many other instances, contact other organizations that have used the trainers and get their assessment.

Cost of training. There are two different types of costs that must be considered as training is assessed. One is the very real expense of training that is charged against the staff development, automation, or personnel budget. The other is an indirect and often untraceable expense that results from time taken away from the regular work routines.

It is possible that the only person that actually needs to be sent for outside training will be the local area network administrator. The existing knowledge and experience of the network administrator will to a significant degree determine the nature and extent of vendor training he or she will need. As the local area network expands, becomes more complex, and as a more diverse array of network peripherals is installed, the administrator will almost certainly need additional training or an updating of acquired skills. As the network expands, it is possible that vendor training will be appropriate for the group of assistants the local area network administrator may have assembled. The need for training the administrator is probably understandable in the minds of most library directors and other individuals who control the purse strings. Even so, there will always be the nagging question of when additional training is unjustified.

Not so comprehensible is the need for widespread training among the library staff if they are to be effective users of the local area network. In general terms, this assignment belongs to the network administrator, but there are a number of expenses attached to training the staff. First, a decision has to be made regarding the teaching aids that are available in the marketplace. There are a variety of videotapes, workbooks, and other instructional materials of varying quality that can be selected to make the learning process more interesting and, perhaps, more successful. Second, regardless of the number of staff trained, there will be a need to keep the individuals up-to-date regarding changes in the network and networking in general. This means subscriptions to a variety of publications ranging from periodicals to newsletters to tabloids. Third, the most difficult cost to address is the cost of missed work. Successful training requires the staff to be away from their workstations in a separate training classroom. Who will perform their work while they are in training? Will the training be done during regular working hours or will it take place after the work day? If it is done after hours, will library staff receive additional compensation for the time spent in training? Whatever the approach, it is an added cost to the expense of making the network operational. If there is a separate training room properly set up, a decision will have to be made regarding whether the local area network will be replicated on a small scale or will it be reconstructed temporarily every time there is a training session.

Time requirements. There is no way to quantify the time required for training. The time the local area network administrator spends attending vendor-sponsored workshops and seminars can be easily identified. In the first year, the network administrator may spend a minimum of two weeks to a month involved in vendor-supported training. In addition, there are untold hours of individualized learning the LAN administrator must pursue on his/her own. These hours are squeezed in among the crises attending the implementation of the network; the direction the learning takes is influenced by the very crises that are taking place.

The remainder of the library staff should be trained only to the minimal level of knowledge they must have in order to utilize the network to support their work. Do not overtrain them. The last thing a library needs is a number of individuals trained to the level of network supervisors without the assignment to function in that role. Mischief will result as they try to put their knowledge to practical use.

The problem with training library staff is that everyone will bring a different level of knowledge and commitment to the training experience. Some people will pick up the training very quickly, be able to demonstrate their competence, and return to their workstation. Other staff members will come as computer illiterates and remain in that condition after hours of training. The assumption is that all staff are capable of learning how to use a local area network and its resources, but this assumption may be sorely tested in practice. The answer to this quandary may be found in individualized instruction rather than group sessions. The best motivation to expedite training and ensure its effectiveness may be to write into staff descriptions the level of knowledge expected and the range of skills to be demonstrated.

Capacity of staff to learn new skills. As mentioned in the previous paragraph, one of the challenges in training library staff is the variance in computer skills and in understanding that are brought to the training environment. The fact that someone has had years of experience as an OCLC terminal operator does not ensure the ability to cope successfully with the functionality of a local area network.

The local area network administrator must try to identify the different capacities of staff members for acquiring new skills. If the library is large enough to have a personnel officer or staff development librarian, that person can be a major ally in assessing the level of computing skills and the learning capacity that each staff member has. One important quality that should be sought in all staff, including the network support staff, is a willingness to spend the time to learn. This willingness must be more than a readiness to attend classes or seminars. There must be a willingness to spend time learning on one's own. It probably can't be over-emphasized that training takes place not only in the formal classroom environment but at each person's personal computer or workstation. A supervisor may think a staff member is "playing around" at his/her workstation when the person actually is exploring how a particular piece of software works and what its true capabilities may be. To be really beneficial, the willingness to explore the software needs to be matched with a willingness to read the manuals and documentation. While the quality of documentation varies greatly, there is no question that it may be the only place where the clues to the potential of the software or the network can be found. Properly presented network training may open a new window for some staff changing their perspective on their job and its place in the library.

Location of training. Initially, at least, training should not take place at the staff member's workstation. The introduction to the local area network and the necessary training should occur in a classroom specially set up for that purpose. There should be a workstation for each person taking the training. This is one of the reasons that training groups should be kept small, no more than 4-6 workstations. The classroom should provide a network that mirrors in miniature the network in the larger organization. It is important, though, to make the learning environment as realistic as possible. This means the staff should use their own data for some of the training. Let it be live. Always assure them that they cannot really damage the network.

The classroom or training room should be away from distractions of the department, and once staff have begun their training, interruptions from the workplace should not be allowed to interfere. Most important of all, there should be no telephones. The classroom should be set up so that the instructor can present instruction on a large screen television or monitor that permits all members of the group to see what is happening. While the instruction should follow a prescribed agenda, there should be sufficient flexibility in the presentation to permit the staff to raise all the questions they wish. Training sessions should probably be no more than one or two hours in length on alternating days, thus permitting staff to return to their regular routine and attempt to make use of the things they have learned. If the trained personnel are available, a team approach in the training is beneficial. The second trainer's contribution comes from walking around the room to make sure no one gets totally lost and then discouraged.

One-time versus ongoing training. In the world of local area networking, there is no such thing as one-time training. Most local area networks will grow and add new staff so quickly that their training will be an ongoing challenge. At the same time, as the network expands its coverage, it will grow in terms of additional features. This will require bringing staff who have already been trained back into the classroom for additional training. Since there is sufficient staff turnover in most libraries, there will be a constant flow of newly employed staff who will need training, too. A question is certain to arise regarding when new staff should be trained. Should they be trained before they are fully acquainted with their primary job assignment? Can they successfully complete training in their primary job assignment without being trained to use the local area network?

One thing is evident: the local area network administrator will have to devote a regular portion of time to training activities. There will also be an enormous demand for informal, very individualized, training that occurs on a spontaneous basis when the network administrator is out in the library. Some of the very best training opportunities occur in this accidental manner. This may be the most important reason for the local area network administrator to spend a portion of each day walking around in the organization. Unless it is convenient to approach the network administrator--and often to do so in private--the staff member, quite often, will not take the time to get the answer that would make the use of the network more effective.

Training needs analysis. In the best of all possible worlds, a needs analysis should be done before any training is undertaken. The problem with this approach is that few, if any, local area network administrators are equipped to engage in this assessment. It may even be problematic in the larger libraries which have a personnel or staff development librarian with the skills to carry out this type of analysis. This is an area in which the library will be well-served to have a vendor or consultant assist in an assessment of the types of training that would benefit the staff.

The challenge in training is to remember to train sufficiently but not to such an extent that staff are distracted from their purpose within the organization. If a needs analysis will help in this respect, then do the analysis.

Feedback from staff about the training. Training will not be successful without feedback from the staff. One of the worst possible scenarios is an exceptionally effective local area network administrator who is a dismal teacher. Unless the person is an effective teacher, all the knowledge in the world about local area networking may be worthless. Library administration and the network administrator need to know whether staff are being trained successfully and whether those training dollars are being spent effectively.

In order to obtain objective feedback, the library administrator may have to develop an outside source to conduct the evaluation of the training sessions. It is important to impress upon the staff that feedback will remain anonymous and that there is a sincere desire on the part of the library administration to determine whether or not staff are benefiting from the process. If the local area network administrator needs some instruction to improve his/her teaching skills, the library administration should be prepared to support it. This commitment should extend to assembling the appropriate instructional aids and materials to make the effort successful. There are individuals who would contend that it is more important to find a person who is a good teacher and train them to be the network administrator than vice versa. Each library has to resolve this quandary.

Confronting staff fears. A number of widespread fears or concerns have to be addressed to ensure successful training experiences. First, there is the fear of automation or personal computing. Many staff still believe that they are incapable of learning the secrets of computing. Their vision of computing is based on the mainframe programmer world filled with engineers who talk a special language that no one else understands. A major task is letting staff know that the personal computer and network user world is very different from the stereotypical view that is often held.

Second, there is a fear of keyboarding. Considering how long the typewriter has been in use, it is amazing how many staff either do not know how to type (keyboard) or are very uncomfortable doing so. Part of the training process may involve providing the opportunity for staff to learn keyboarding or improve the level of skill they have. Also, if this is not part of each and every job description, it should be, immediately.

Third, there is a fear of appearing foolish or incompetent in front of one's peers. Each of us has a perception of how we are viewed by our co-workers, and anything that tends to diminish that image is a threat. Training to use the local area network can be an enormous threat to staff who have become very comfortable in their work routines. The prospect of having to learn a new set of skills can be unsettling at best and life threatening at worst. The local area network administrator, supported by the library administration, must establish the training process as a non-threatening experience in which staff are given an opportunity to learn at the pace that is best for each of them. This does not mean that the administration abdicates the responsibility to set standards and goals for the training. It does mean demonstrating a capacity to adapt to individual learning speeds while maintaining performance expectations.

A coordinate issue to the concern about fears is the matter of training library administrators. This may be the most challenging part of all the training activities the local area network administrator is involved in. Given human nature, the network administrator should anticipate that the director and/or other top-level administrators will not want to parade their level of incompetence when it comes to computer skills, keyboarding, and quickness to learn new skills. Whether it is legitimate to engage in individualized training for the library administration depends upon local circumstances but there may be no other option available to the local area network administrator. It is absolutely critical that the library administration publicly demonstrate their support of the training programs and there is no better way to confirm this commitment than taking part in them.

Another aspect of the training issue relates to the matter of documentation. Typically, improvement in the quality of documentation usually occurs as staff work through the process of implementing the network. There is a concomitant concern about the ability of the documentation to support the training of staff. At the very least, the documentation should be usable enough so that those staff members who will be supporting the local area network administrator can use it for their self-education. Ideally, the documentation should be written in such a way that the network administrator can use it as a base on which the training program for the rest of the staff can be built.

While there is an obvious set of goals for the training of staff to use the local area network, there is a broader, more intangible set of organizational attitudes that should be affected by the training process if possible. Specifically, a desired outcome is the creation of a willingness among staff to spend time learning more about networking, personal computing, and their own jobs. Throughout the training experience, there should be an emphasis on the importance of taking an exhaustive look at the way in which work has been done to determine if there are better ways of achieving the same ends. If staff can be instilled with this attitude, then local area networking can hold real opportunity for significant improvements in productivity and the delivery of new services.

Costs

If thorough preparatory work has been done during the design/selection phase, then, perhaps, with some luck, the cost projections were accurate and there have been no surprises. Most libraries are not so fortunate. A distinction that appears in information about local area networks is that between "hard" and "soft" costs. Hard costs include the obvious items: cable, servers, PCs, printers, and such. Soft costs include a number of obvious items such as installation, training, repair, and maintenance. There are a number of additional items that are consistently overlooked. Often there will be a need to modify existing furniture or acquire new furniture as the network is brought into an office. Even if no new furniture is needed, inevitably there will be a need to rearrange offices and workspace which may result in a need for modifications of some type. At the very least, there will be lost work time from the interruptions in the daily work routine.

Another soft cost is the assortment of manuals that are needed to support the local area network. Does each staff member have a full set of the appropriate training manuals and other documentation, or do the staff share them? Then there are procedure and policy manuals; again, one per person, one per workstation, or some other arrangement. Software documentation falls into the same category, one per person or per workstation. How many copies of the locally created network documentation should there be? Regardless of the choice that is made, it can be guaranteed there will never be quite enough, and staff will never be quite satisfied. The costs will continue to mount, however.

The "bottom line" of the cost aspect of a local area network is the problem that all libraries face: non-recurring versus recurring costs. Most of the "hard" costs mentioned above can be covered with non-recurring funds. Using non-recurring funds for equipment replacement or the addition of new equipment will always be a problem because there is no guarantee, of course, of their availability from year to year. Funding recurring costs present a more serious challenge because most library budgets are not growing in a manner that will accommodate the addition of a significant new set of continuing expenses. The result is that each of the existing budget lines is pared slightly to create the needed pool of funding required to support the new costs.

Installation with NOVELL

Some final very practical thoughts about installation are presented in the context of NOVELL installation, but are relevant in various ways to other network operating software. It is important to emphasize that having experience in installing a word processing program is not an adequate prerequisite for installing network software. More important is an understanding of how the network will work and how the software will interact with the various pieces of hardware on the network. During the installation process the software will prompt for answers to a large number of questions. Choosing the correct answers to these questions is critical to a successful installation. NOVELL, at least, provides many work forms that are very helpful in this process. Take the time to complete them. Checklists in the documentation can be invaluable if used.

Installation of NOVELL's software on a server varies from environment to environment with many options that can be selected at many stages in the process and which can change the final result. The following facts may influence whether an installation is undertaken without help. NOVELL version 2.15C, for the 286 computer, is packaged in a set of forty disks. One of the first questions is the method of installation to be used--a terrible question for the first-time installer. Installing the network using floppy disks, as most users do initially, will require a minimum of an hour trading floppy disks in the server. There is documentation to help with this endeavor--a lot of documentation. While the NOVELL documentation is very good, it would require an even greater number of volumes to cover all the information and options that might be possible. It is important to read all of the documentation before any installation is begun.

NOVELL's 386-based software has been greatly improved in terms of the amount of disk swapping that is required. Its original release of this software contained only nine disks, although later versions have increased that number.

Certainly, the first-time networker can proceed alone, but it is far better to seek out others in the area that have installed a network before and ask for help. Read all of the documentation, not in a manner to remember the detail but to get a sense of the process and when and where the options will arise for selection. This will allow the installer to gain a base of understanding about the network and absorb some of the vocabulary peculiar to networking. Before beginning the actual installation, make a copy of all the disks to be used and file the originals away somewhere out of sight. Use the copies for the installation; DO NOT USE THE ORIGINALS. Use the installation manual turning it page by page as the questions and options appear on the screen. This will be quietly reassuring as the process unfolds. Perhaps the most reassuring way to install the network is to make it a two-person project. At times it is comforting to have someone to talk to and who will recall which options were chosen. Remember to document each of the options selected. If Netware 286 is being used, it may be helpful to sort the disks alphabetically to facilitate finding the appropriate disk. Do all of this in a "mini-network" configuration of one server and one workstation. Identifying problems and arriving at solutions will be much easier in this limited arrangement.

Turning the Network Over For Use

Finally, the installation process reaches a point at which you must review what you have done and then release the local area network for general library-wide use. If the design work and recommendations of the vendors have been utilized, the following sequence should be able to be identified and traced through the installation process.[6]

1. Set up the server and workstation hardware.
2. Make sure the combination works stand-alone.
3. Install the network cards and cables and connect them.
4. Install the system software on the server and test it.
5. Install the system software on the workstation and test it.
6. Bring up your applications and test them.

Testing the network, in all its aspects and functions, becomes the critical last step. Test from the central equipment and each of the PCs that are attached to the network. Test every possible combination and permutation of activities and functions that you can imagine, because the unimaginable will occur. As a rule, the following tests should be done:[7]

- Test all file transfer capabilities with all supported file types (Most networks support sequential file access, but others support relative files and indexed files as well. Test them all).
- Test all file types with the various operating systems. Make sure that all possible combinations are tested.
- If the network supports it, try sending multiple files to a single node simultaneously to test network synchronization and access.
- If virtual terminal software is provided, try connecting to the various systems and exercise all aspects of the link software (screen editing, forms, graphics, etc....)
- Write some sample network programs to test the network applications libraries as well as to verify the programmability of the network for future applications.
- Put any network control utilities through the paces. Use them in a typical environment. Try to break the network. The users will.
- If any applications you are currently using claim to support the LAN you have selected, test them as well.
- Disconnect nodes and verify network stability.

When all of the testing is done, begin to bring the library staff onto the network a few at a time. Workgroups probably make the most sense because they will immediately have reason to begin to communicate with one another and share files. As each workgroup achieves a level of stability, bring on the next.

5

LAN Implementation

Once the local area network is physically installed with all the workstations and peripherals connected, the challenge of actually "implementing" the network begins. In reality, this should be another part of the seamless movement from identifying what is needed for a library's network to having it fully operational, integrated into the activities of the library. This part of the sequence involves policies and procedures, functioning applications, continued training, and resolving unanticipated problems with equipment.

As the network begins to function, the first indications of whether network capacity and user needs were properly forecast will occur in the form of an overwhelming number of problems confronting the network administrator and staff. Incompatible hardware, insufficient capacity in the hardware, and inappropriate media decisions will begin to affect the ability of the network to respond to the demands being placed upon it. These physical problems with the network may be difficult and frustrating to confront and solve, but they will be many times easier than the personnel problems that surface from failed training or unanticipated changes in the library's organization. The network administrator should not plan to be absent for some time after the network is officially operating. No matter how complex or simple the system is, there is always a need to hand-hold or simply answer questions.

Although the library has planned as well as it can for the network and has provided training for staff who will be using the network, the staff reaction to all of this effort may not become apparent until implementation begins. It is possible that some library staff will be pathologically afraid of being displaced from their jobs. Others may be unwilling to make the commitment of time and energy to learn the new skills, policies, and procedures required to make the network function. Still others may resist change because they can see their positions of formal or informal power and influence in the library changing.

All the skills of the network administrator, supported by the power and influence of the library administration, may be needed to overcome the staff-related reluctance to accept the network. No single action will win over

those staff members in opposition to change; many different actions
employed consistently and equitably over an extended period of time will be
successful. Some suggestions:

- Be absolutely certain that staff whose assignments are affected
  by the network have a thorough understanding of the new
  responsibilities that they will have and that the new responsibilities are clearly stated.
- Be consistent in informing all library staff of the changes that
  are occurring and the effects for the library.
- Ensure that library staff have the opportunity to acquire new
  skills, knowledge and abilities to fully implement and use the
  network and its components in addition to training for the network.

As was emphasized in the last chapter, plan the manner in which the
library staff will be brought on to the network. If it is not already known,
identify those departments or workgroups within the library that are either
the most technologically adept or most enthusiastic about the prospect of
local area networking. Begin the implementation with those staff members.
Their enthusiasm can be contagious within the library and other staff will be
far more responsive to them than to the library administration. As each
workgroup of staff achieves a satisfactory level of skill with the network
functions, move on to the next group. It is conceivable that staff members
recently trained may be the most effective prospective mentors for experiencing the network for the first time.

An early task in implementing the local area network is confidence
building. Staff members must believe in the ability of the network to
achieve the objectives that were established. An obstacle to this will be the
reliability of the network. All networks will fail; but if the local area
network is released to library staff before it is properly stabilized and
debugged, library staff will be extremely reluctant to integrate it into their
routines. Even after the network is stabilized and debugged, failure is an
ever-present threat.

The network administrator should have worked out the necessary
procedures, shared them with all appropriate staff, and trained those needing
training so that network failure can be reduced and time lost minimized.
When a PC or a branch of a network has failed, it is simply wise planning
to have staff who can respond in a short time to remove the PC or
disconnect the branch so that the remainder of the network can continue to
operate. Naturally, there will be some network failures that will require
technicians who have been trained in network repair and maintenance. The
matter of network failure, especially of centralized equipment, is something
that NOVELL has devoted considerable attention to in its network software.

Guaranteed network operation is a very difficult issue. In its netware NOVELL has created a number of safeguards to ensure the network remains online and backedup.

Network Failure

Networks, like most electronic systems, can fail for any number of reasons. There appear to be two different kinds of network failure. First, there is the total server error when the server itself has a problem. This can result from a variety of causes. It may be the result of a hard disk crash, the power to the server may have been corrupted or interrupted, or the software on the server may have been changed. These are just a few of the possible causes.

NOVELL and other hardware vendors have made it easier to avoid this type of failure. One common method of protecting information on a server's disk is by "disk mirroring." This technique is done by simply matching the server's hard disk with a second. The result is two hard disks of the same size in the server. No additional storage space is gained in this installation. Each time a user writes to the server and the information is saved to disk, the information is saved to the second disk too, "mirroring" the first disk. This is an excellent method of assuring that the information will be stored, and even if one of the disks fails, the data can be retrieved from the "mirror" disk. The disadvantage of this approach is that it can be quite costly if large-capacity hard disks are involved.

Another common way to protect the data on a server is called "hot fix." This involves an area that is set up when the network software is initially installed, for the network to use. If the network software determines that a portion of the space the server is using is failing, the data are written to the hot fix area and the failed portion of the disk is marked as unusable.

While the topic of electrical power will be addressed later in this chapter, it is relevant to server failures, too. The importance of clean, uninterrupted power cannot be over-emphasized. Power conditioners are available that clean the local electrical power for use on the network. UPSs (uninterruptable power supplies) have been available for the past three years to provide servers and other key machines with the ability to function even after all power has been cut. These UPSs work on a battery-based system and can provide power to a connected server or other equipment for an extended period of time that is determined by the amount of battery time that has been purchased. A drawback to these UPSs is that often the purchaser doesn't understand what is being protected. For example, if the power fails in a library and the network server has a battery backup, it is true the server can maintain its functionality until the battery runs down. What of the workstations on the network? If the workstations are to remain functional, each PC would have to be supported by its own UPS. This may seem to be a minor point, but all too often library staff believe that the UPS protecting the server is also protecting their individual workstations. This won't be the case when the power fails.

A number of vendors, including NOVELL, manufacture servers with a UPS as an integral part of the unit. This provides even more protection than the power conditioner type of UPS. With this equipment, when the server loses power it sends a signal to all user stations notifying them of the power loss and the fact that the server will shut down in a specified period of time. After that period of time, which varies based on the capacity of the batteries, the server will close all of its files in an orderly manner and actually shut the network down. This approach helps to eliminate the open file errors that can occur when a standard UPS runs out of power. While this option provides an improved level of insurance, the servers equipped in this fashion do cost more.

The second type of network failure is much more common, unfortunately, because it involves the network cabling. This is usually fixed much more easily but can still be very trying. Most networks will experience this type of failure with some degree of regularity. Locating the cabling problem will be the challenge for networking staff. Typically, there will be high levels of stress on the staff to find this type of problem as quickly as possible. In these situations, the importance of adequate documentation and wiring diagrams is realized.

Cabling failures can occur for a variety of reasons, ranging from library staff members who want to clean their desk so they unhook their workstations from the network, to electricians who installed fire alarm equipment on the network wiring. Over time, each library will develop its volume of "can you believe it" situations that caused the network to fail.

Software Applications

Although the question of software applications should have been raised during the design phase, the effect that the various software applications may have on a local area network will become evident during implementation. The first issue that must be addressed is the diversity of applications that will be permitted on the network. Whether it is appreciated or not, there will probably have to be a restriction on the number of different software packages allowed on the network. There are several reasons for this. First, acknowledged or not, there will be an expectation that the network administrator will be able to provide support and service for all the software found on the network. Second, it is possible that some software applications could be incompatible with certain features of the network that has been installed. Third, it may be more effective for a networked version of a software package to be acquired, replacing all the single user copies that exist in a library. The networked version will generally permit multiple uses of the same files simultaneously. Fourth, it is possible that some applications might have a negative impact on the functionality of the network, loading it down to the point where it is inoperable.

The authors' networking experience supports the approach of one word processing, one spreadsheet, one database, and one communications application for the network. This simplifies training and support processes which can become very difficult as the number of network users grows.

If a staff member has a justifiable reason for retaining a unique software application, it should be made clear that the application resides only on the staff member's PC and is not to be loaded onto the network unless authorized by the network administrator. The staff member should understand, too, that no support will be provided when problems arise with the software. This may seem unreasonable and unnecessarily harsh but any other approach will result in a hodge-podge of software that will be unmanageable.

Electronic Mail

Whether it is one of the features of the networking software or a separate application, electronic mail may be the most significant networking addition to the library. Often, the preliminary reaction to the availability of electronic mail is that it is not needed; existing communications are just fine.

> 'Electronic mail is the generic name for non-interactive communication of text, data, image, or voice messages between a sender and designated recipient by systems utilizing telecommunications link.'
>
> By this definition, there are at least six technologies that qualify as electronic mail: computer mailbox systems, facsimile, voice mail systems, telex, Electronic Data Interchange (EDI), and computer conferencing. . . .[1]

For our purposes electronic mail will encompass only the first of the six technologies--computer mailboxes.

Electronic mail has the potential to alter much of the communication that occurs among library staff. The extent to which that potential is achieved will depend upon the willingness of the library administration and staff to depart from the traditional communication avenues. Frankly, the key will be the library administration. Much of the formal communication that occurs within a library originates with the administration, so there can be an immediate impact. This can be one of the first arenas in which the opportunity for conserving resources, staff, and materials can be seen. Whether it is memos distributed to library staff, minutes of meetings held, announcements, policy statements, or procedures, each of these can be distributed to library staff who are part of the electronic mail system.

It is not necessary that a staff member have his or her own PC in order to take advantage of electronic mail, although it is certainly much more convenient. The most critical consideration is that the staff member have an address or mailbox within the system. If the staff member has a password and rights to log-on to the network, then he/she should be able to send and receive electronic mail from any PC on the network.

There are some unanticipated problems with the use of electronic mail that all library staff may have to accommodate. The first of these is the fact that all the visual clues about personal relationships in an organization are absent from electronic mail. The second is that body language is removed from the interaction, often making it very difficult to anticipate how a message is going to be received. A very innocent spoken message can become offensive when it appears on the computer screen. Third, communication tends to be more informal in electronic mail systems. This can present challenges to the individual or library that has previously functioned in a very formal structure.

These unanticipated problems are overwhelmed by the distinct improvement in the speed with which communications can take place. Phone tag is reduced, if not eliminated. Information can be distributed more quickly and more broadly than ever before. It is possible that effective use of electronic mail will provide the opportunity to consider reducing the number of levels of management that exist in the library. Perhaps, best of all, it can speed up decision making.

These benefits are possible, but they will not happen unless there is a very specific commitment on the part of library administration and staff to utilize the full potential of electronic mail. Electronic mail must be used every day, and it must become second nature to staff. Unless it is the first thing a staff member checks each morning when arriving at work and after returning from lunch, the system will not succeed. If electronic mail doesn't succeed, the local area network is not likely to succeed.

Associated features, as part of the electronic mail application, will often enhance the total package. Calendaring, scheduling of equipment and facilities, arranging meetings, attaching separate files for transmission, personal notes, and to-do-lists are typical features. The result is a computerized time management system that can improve personal and organizational effectiveness.

Regardless of the features of the particular electronic mail system, three things must be done as soon as the network begins to function. First, each person must be assigned a mailbox and be given the training to send and receive mail messages. Second, mail groups must be created to facilitate the library-wide distribution of messages. These groupings can be based on departmental, workgroup, or interest group affiliation. Creating these groups expedites sending messages by eliminating the need to enter the names of large numbers of staff. Third, create the equivalent of a phone book that provides the mail addresses for all library staff and the various distribution groups that have been established. If 80 percent of the library's communications takes place between people within the library, electronic mail can certainly have an enormous impact, saving time and resources and improving decision making.

Documentation

In the last chapter the need to document the installation was discussed. The need to document continues through implementation, in fact, throughout the life of the network. Documentation that was created earlier in the process can provide staff with a basis for making evaluations of whether the network is meeting expectations. Documentation can provide the framework for instructing new employees who join the library after the network is operating.

There are two challenges related to documentation. First, make certain that it is written in a manner that ensures that it will be understood by library staff. There is an almost inescapable temptation to use the jargon associated with networking. Resist. If the documentation is to be useful, it must be understandable. Second, documentation must be kept current. This can become an enormous burden for the network administrator, but it is essential that changes in the network and its operations be recorded and distributed in a timely manner. While manuals need to be within reach of each PC for the documentation, it may be appropriate to use electronic mail to ensure that the information is distributed quickly.

Policies and Procedures

The freewheeling world of personal computing stands in dramatic contrast to the local area networking environment. Stand-alone PCs permit the user to have an unbelievable degree of independence in terms of how the equipment is arranged, the software applications that can be used, data entry, security, and backing up files. The same degree of independence simply will not work in a local area network. The interdependence of network users is so significant that small oversights can cause catastrophic results to everyone.

One way, and perhaps the only way, to protect against these network problems is to establish network policies and procedures that apply without exception to all network users. Many of these policies and procedures cannot be open for debate and discussion as they are formulated, thus reemphasizing the fact that, in contrast to many library activities, participatory decision making is not useful. This is why the network administrator must have the complete unequivocal support of the library administration to ensure that the network operation will be successful.

Examples of the various subjects for which policies and procedures need to be established include:

- moving of network equipment, including PC equipment
- introduction of external data to the network from floppy disks brought in from outside the library (viruses)
- application software other than that approved for use on the network
- schedule for clearing out electronic mailboxes and removing other files from personal directories
- deleting files thought not to be in use
- the size of personal work areas on the server hard disk
- hours when each workstation can be used
- open sharing of passwords
- whether two terminals should be used by the same staff member at the same time
- level of rights given to staff members

Policies and procedures must be kept up to date, regardless of the number, and reflect the changing level of sophistication that library staff will acquire over time. As a network administrator works with the problems and frustrations of network operation, it is easy to lose sight of the overall improvement in staff ability to make use of the network.

Internetworking

The ability to connect with other networks may have been one of the original concerns reflected in the design of the local area network. If it was not, it will certainly develop into a concern as soon as library staff attain a minimal level of competency. Several questions will have to be examined and resolved from a technical standpoint before internetworking will be feasible:

- What protocols are used on the networks to be accessed?
- What types of service exist?
- What methods of addressing the other networks are available?
- What data rates and units are used?
- What is the gateway medium?
- What is the access method that can be used?
- What networks do the library staff need to access?
- Are there additional fees or charges that must be paid in order to gain access?

Since internetworking promises to be important in the years ahead, it should be planned for from the beginning of the library's involvement in local area networking. The absence of extensive documentation, standardization, and rate of change in the regional and national networking environment reinforce the importance of developing adequate expertise with the local area network before embarking on internetworking.

Organizational Structure

Libraries display a wide variety of organizational structures, from the traditional extremely hierarchical organization to the very flat. Libraries that have been centralized organizationally may find that the implementation of a local area network begins to destabilize the historic arrangement. Local area networks operate on the philosophy that intelligence and information will be widely dispersed throughout the organization. New channels of communication are automatically available as the network becomes operational, and the consequence is an inability to exercise any effective central control. The result may be that radically different avenues for decision making begin to take shape in the library displacing the management-driven approaches that have traditionally dominated library operation.

Security

Security is an aspect of local area networking that is easily overlooked. The operating philosophy of a local area network is to facilitate the sharing of information. Balanced against both the operating philosophy of local area networking and the library's reason for being--that information should be broadly available--is the fact that data must be protected for reasons of privacy, confidentiality, and the investment committed to creating or assembling the information. Most organizations, including libraries, have gotten used to the idea that equipment resources must be protected. The concept of extending similar protection to the information is not as broadly embedded. The reality of "white-collar" crime that causes information to be manipulated, reprogrammed, altered, or stolen, is painful for institutions such as libraries.

Libraries should be especially sensitive to copyright as a security issue. Once the appropriate rights have been given to a staff member, that person can download data files and application software to their own hard disk or floppy disks depending upon the hardware configuration. The staff member's need should be clearly identified and agreed upon before rights are established on the network. The library administration should have established clearly stated policies regarding the legality of using network software on non-networked machines in the library or staff member's homes.

Physical

Security for the physical network is an obvious concern and is an extension of concern for all library equipment. The more difficult security concern relates to the security of the data being stored on the network. A natural reaction is to question what in the data stored on the local area network could be sensitive enough to raise concerns about unauthorized access? If the library's network has budget data, personnel information, planning information, or patron information, there may be someone who is interested in looking at or copying the information. At the very least, or worst, there may be someone--a hacker, perhaps--who is interested in just wreaking havoc in the network. Whatever the threat to the data the library has on the network, security is a concern that must be considered from the time of the initial discussions about local area networking.

There are eight types of LAN security in general use today: physical security, call-back security, passwords and user IDs, directory and file access rights, diskless workstations, measures to reduce electromagnetic radiation from cables and computers, security based on proprietary disk formats, and security provided by applications.[2]

The concerns about the physical security of the network can be divided between those related to the servers, PCs, printers, modems, etc., and those related to the wiring plant. In terms of servers, etc., the best approach is to limit physical access to the equipment. Realistically, this is sometimes practical and other times impractical. The server and supporting equipment should be located out of the way, in a space that can be locked by key or combination. One of the difficult questions for library staff to answer is whether the security threats are more internal or external. The answer to this question will influence the steps that must be taken. A factor that should be considered in this examination is the threat from the well-intentioned but badly equipped staff member who thinks he or she can fix a server problem or similar difficulty and save the networking staff time. This person is just as much a security threat as someone who tries to physically remove the server.

Physical security for workstations offers another challenge. Even if the workstations are in locked individual offices should additional precautions such as locked keyboard covers and lockable shields for the other pieces of the workstation be taken? If workstations or PCs are in open work areas, the diskless workstation may provide protection against unauthorized use of the equipment to access the network. The need for particular library staff to download information will influence the ability to use diskless workstations. There is a status factor related to diskless workstations that cannot be ignored. Often, staff will conclude that a diskless PC is an indication that they do not have the skills or competency to use a "real" PC. While it may be concluded that physical security is not a practical alternative, the use of of protection at other levels may have to be explored.

Earlier in the book, there was some discussion of how secure each type of wiring media was. Twisted pair, shielded or not, is unquestionably the easiest to tap. Whether a physical tap is applied or the radio frequency transmission is intercepted, the task is neither difficult nor complicated. Compounding the problem with this media is the fact that intrusion into the network could go undetected unless the library is willing to install fairly sophisticated detection equipment or employ encryption techniques to protect the data.

Coaxial cable is little better than twisted pair. Tapping the cable can be accomplished in an unobtrusive manner that can go undetected. Intercepting the transmission signals without a tap is more difficult but, certainly, not impossible. The best protection is found using fiber optic media. It has been assumed that this media was next to impossible to tap and that, without a tap, picking up the transmission signals could not be done. Unfortunately, it is possible to tap fiber optic cable, but detection of the tap is probably easier.

A final comment related to the physical network. While nearly everyone focuses on the wiring and the equipment, another part of the physical network should be protected in some way: the assortment of circuit breakers, fuses, power lines, transformers, and such, that provide electrical power to the network. Nothing is more frustrating than a network failure that is caused by utility personnel or other staff who unthinkingly turn off the power without checking with library staff ahead of time. Restricted access to these parts of the networked environment, with established policies accepted and enforced by all bodies interacting with the library, can avoid a large number of problems.

Passwords

After the decisions have been made regarding physical security, the next step is to institute log-on security or passwords. This facet of security will reveal how committed the library staff is to the concept of protecting network information and restricting access to the network.

Typically, each individual should be assigned a user ID or name and a password. The user ID does not necessarily have to be held in confidence the same way the password should be. Often the user ID can be some shortened version of the user's full name. The password is another matter. This is the key that will allow the individual onto the network and, in combination with access rights which will be discussed later, determines what they are permitted to do on the network. All too often, the network user will pick some easily remembered word, name, or short set of numbers, letters, or a combination. The result is that an intruder can easily deduce or extract the password. Passwords should be six or seven digits or characters in length. The complaint that it is hard to remember is simply not acceptable. Many times staff will compromise the password that has been selected by posting their password on the PC or by sharing it with their co-workers in the office.

A classic example of this situation is the library administrative office in which all the office staff, including administrators, use the password posted by one of the secretaries so they can work on a conveniently located workstation. The result is that when problems occur at that workstation, it is impossible to determine who is responsible because everyone is working through one person's password.

Network software, today, offers additional levels of protection to the password if the network administrator chooses to use them. NOVELL Netware provides these options. A time limit may be set on the validity of a password, requiring that it be changed on a predetermined schedule. A warning is given to the network user, beginning a specified number of days before the password is invalidated, that a new password must be established. Another feature limits knowledge of the password to only the individual and not the network administrator, too. There is a problem with this approach if the individual fails to remember the password; another has to be assigned because the network administrator cannot go into the system and discover what the lost password is. It is possible to restrict the password to a set number of characters, eliminating the use of family names and other easily discovered possibilities.

The "bottom line" with passwords rests with instilling in all library staff the commitment that the passwords are confidential information and not to be shared with their co-workers. Network administrators need to have this philosophy reinforced by library administrators.

Call-Back

Even if the library's local area network does not begin its operation with a remote access feature, it will eventually acquire the capability. While it is often important for individuals outside the library to be able to call in, this provides the possibility for a break in the library network's security. A method known as "call-back" security has been developed to provide a screening mechanism to minimize unauthorized outside access to the network. Typically, a remote user will call into the network and key in his/her user ID and password. The network receives that information and hangs up the call. Network software does a check of its tables to determine whether there is a registered user with the received user ID and password. If there is, the table will contain the person's phone number, and the network will call the remote user and reestablish the network link. Unless the unauthorized individual is calling from the previously authorized phone number, possession of the user ID and password will not be sufficient to enter the network. This feature, or some variation, will become increasingly important in the future as remote access grows in importance.

Access Rights

Directory and file access rights offer another level of protection to the networks, its applications, and information. There are several levels or variations to access rights: the file server, directories, files, and the user. It should be evident that only a few network users will ever need to do more than access the file server; the capacity to change the file server environment should be held by only one or two people in the library. Whether a network user should be able to create directories, modify those directories, or determine the amount of data they will store in a directory are factors that most networked organizations will allow a network administrator to determine. It is reasonable to assume that the answers to these concerns would vary among the network users. Finally, with regard to file security, most network software permits the network administrator to specify file attributes for each user. These attributes determine whether a user can read, write, open, delete, modify, execute, search, or create files in a directory.

Parallel to server, directory, and file access rights, NOVELL Netware provides user rights. These are called "trustee rights," but can be associated with a user on an individual basis, as a member of a user group, or in comparison with another individual or group. These rights are the same as the attributes specified in the preceding paragraph. The result of these layers of access rights is that an intruder who does acquire an ID and password and enters the network will be restricted to the "rights" level assigned to the network user.

The process of learning "trustee rights" and levels of security within a network can be confusing and frustrating as a network becomes operational. It is fair to say that a network can never be too safe. There is nothing more frustrating than to find important files have been erased and no one admits to doing it. One approach that seems to work is to create a directory for each staff member that only that person has rights to. This probably protects the staff member's files best. The staff member can accurately be told that no one without the staff member's password could have erased or tampered the files. This arrangement makes it much easier for the system administrator to impress upon library staff the importance of keeping their passwords secure.

Diskless workstations were mentioned earlier, but deserve an additional comment. Inevitably some networked PCs or workstations cannot be placed where access is restricted. In those instances, diskless PCs offer a level of protection against unauthorized downloading of information or uploading material. The diskless PC is an attractive alternative for those staff who are involved with data entry and nothing more.

Backing Up

If security on the library's network is breached and information is lost or destroyed, the ease of restoring that information will be determined by whether or not backing up the network has been standard practice. One of the liabilities of the personal computing environment is the mind-set that determines that it is the other person who loses his/her data. Until an individual or organization sustains a major loss of data, it may be impossible to convince them that the expense of installing the backup equipment is a wise investment. Backup systems, especially tape backup, have dropped substantially in price and can be installed with little difficulty. Often the process can be automated to the point where it requires minimal human intervention. The admonition has to be "don't put off backing up." If you do, you will pay a substantial price to restore your databases of information.

6
LAN Operation

As important as the selection, installation, and implementation of a local area network may be, the crucial element in the entire adoption process is whether or not the library can ensure that the network will function effectively enough that staff can actually begin to integrate the network into the work routines. Network operation must become an inseparable aspect of library operation if the advantages of networking are to be utilized. The fact that the library's network administrator has been successful thus far does not guarantee long-term success. Routines for the day-to-day management of the network have to be identified, established, and accepted.

The complexity of network management finally becomes apparent as the network becomes an integral part of the library's operations. To be successful, network management has to include the following broad areas of concern:

- monitoring network performance
- identifying network problems
- solving network problems
- renewing and expanding the network
- monitoring network configuration
- planning for network expansion

While the focus of network management tends toward the hardware and software aspects, there is a major need to remember the human side of networking. If the personnel aspects are lost sight of or forgotten, the most perfectly installed local area network may still fail.

Monitoring Network Performance

There is no question that monitoring the performance of the local area network is important. A legitimate question to ask is, how much is enough? While there is no standardized response to the question, there may be some guidelines that can be useful to help library staff determine what is reasonable. If the network encompasses only a few individuals in a limited number of units or workgroups with a restricted amount of equipment, then monitoring may be able to be conducted without much in the way of additional software or hardware. The larger and more complex the network and the more indispensable it is to the work of the library, the more important monitoring will become. In that situation, the investment in sufficiently sophisticated software and hardware is a necessity.

NOVELL Netware, for example, includes some monitoring software as part of its operating system. It is wise for a systems administrator to become familiar with this package and use it on a regular basis. One of NOVELL's software programs is called FCONSOLE. Using this, the network can be examined while it is running. FCONSOLE enables the system administrator to locate potential problems by monitoring the hard disk and memory located in the server. An experienced system operator can use this program to determine if the hard disk is close to failure or if the network is operating close to capacity.

While this is just one example of the monitoring software that is available and what it can do, it is possible to invest a substantial amount of money and time in extremely sophisticated monitoring programs. It is important to ensure the reliability of the network but, in the last analysis, the library administration with the advice of the network administrator will have to decide when enough is enough. If a library is using a sophisticated Ethernet network there is a very expensive software program, LANALYZER, that will actually check the performance of all the Ethernet cards on the network. Although expensive, for a certain type of network this software might be a bargain in terms of problems prevented.

Regardless of the size or complexity of the network, it is possible to bury the library with the task of collecting data. This will inevitably turn out to be a waste of scarce resources of time and equipment. Determine whether you really need to know who is using the network, how long or how often they are using the network, whether there are attempts to by-pass security, what the use of various applications is, and when the use is heaviest.

An aspect of monitoring network performance that is often forgotten involves getting out and talking with network users. Do not talk to sophisticated users alone; talk with all types of users. They may alert the administrator to a problem before it is reflected by the monitoring equipment or in the use statistics for the network. Talking to the network users also reinforces the perception that network administrators are interested in the concerns and ideas that network users have.

Do not depend on the network users to take advantage of established reporting procedures the library may have developed. Likewise, do not depend on the users to initiate conversations with the systems administrator. Too often, library staff do not want to have others consider them "dumb" so they will not complain or seek answers to the questions they have. Informal, off-the-record conversations can reduce the frustration level among users and, gradually, build their level of confidence so they will not be reluctant to raise questions and concerns.

Identifying and Solving Network Problems

There is no question that the library will have problems with its local area network; the only questions are when and how severe the problems will be. Whether the library decided during the selection process to have a vendor supply maintenance and repair services or to perform these tasks with library staff, some minimal-level activities can be carried out by library network staff. Maintenance should be interpreted as those activities that help prevent problems from occurring. These activities may not always be successful, but they will not hurt. Repair includes the activities necessary to correct a problem that has taken place. Sometimes in the process of performing maintenance functions, substantial problems are created for the network. Whether maintenance or repair work is being performed, the immediate result may be downtime for the network.

Network downtime will take place. Too many things can cause network problems. Software malfunctions, power surges, failure of parts, dip switches that need to be reset--all can cause network crashes. If a network crash does occur, the network administrator should have a developed policy and set of procedures that go into effect automatically. These should have been reviewed with the library administrator and all other appropriate library staff so that there is an understanding of the steps that will be taken to remedy the problem.

A question that may be raised, in trying to anticipate how network problems should be addressed, is whether the library can afford to have backup equipment on hand to replace existing equipment as soon as the cause of a problem is identified. Although this practice is sometimes followed in the operation of integrated library systems, it is the ILS vendor that carries the investment burden of that additional equipment. When the library is faced with that challenge, the wisdom of some backup equipment may be quickly dismissed as beyond the carrying ability of the budget. The question that more properly should be asked is how long can the library afford to be without a functioning network. If the library administration can place a value on lost time and opportunity, then it may be possible to demonstrate that having backup equipment available will actually save money for the library.

Network configuration was discussed earlier in the book, but as the challenge of identifying and solving network problems is reviewed, the topic is relevant again. When a network problem does occur, the obvious first goal should be to minimize the impact of the problem. If the topology of the network is such that a problem anywhere on the network affects all network users, the library staff could be quickly frustrated. The ideal situation is a topology that permits the affected part of the network to be detached from the rest of the network, permitting it to resume operation.

For example, an ARCNET network will allow problem areas to be removed from the network while the remainder continues to function. A product called a "smart hub" has been developed for this type of network. This hub serves two purposes. First, it is the central connecting point for several PCs or workstations as any hub would be. Second, it is installed with LCDs and software that track errors on each line of the network. This can help reduce downtime in solving problems and in performing regular maintenance. While this type of hub is somewhat more costly, the question that must continually be asked is how important is the insurance against network failure.

Renewing and Expanding the Network

Wear-and-tear on equipment and the changes in library staff are two reasons that renewal and expansion of the network will become a way of life for the network administrator. Equipment requires periodic maintenance or replacement with newer, and usually more powerful, hardware. When that happens, depending upon the network topology, network operation may come to a halt while the exchange occurs. Remember that the networking software may require changes that could range from minimal to extensive if a new piece of equipment is replacing an existing piece. Some of these changes may have to be done at the central file server location and others will have to occur at the individual workstation location. When the work has to be done on the central server, a decision will have to be made regarding taking the network down during the library's open operating hours or waiting until the work day is complete. A library staff new to the demands of local area networking may be reluctant to work beyond the normal work schedule or there may be a reluctance on the part of library administration to absorb the additional budget impact of overtime, but availability and reliability of the network may be the deciding factors in when the work is done.

Adding new users to an existing group of network users may create an additional set of problems. If adequate provisions were not made when the network cabling was done, extra wiring may have to be installed. Even if distances between workstations or PCs can be maintained, the question of whether the network has to be halted to install new pieces of equipment still remains. Some topologies will require downtime, others will not. An earlier decision may return to haunt the daily operation of the network. Will the network software have to be reconfigured to accommodate the new equipment? The answer depends on the network software you have selected.

Discussions of network expansion focus, naturally, on adding additional equipment and running more cable, but there is a human side that must be considered. As the network installation occurred and the first set of network users were introduced to the network, a fixed routine should have been established that covered all the steps needed for a library staff member to use the network. Typically, developing this routine is forgotten. The activities that should be included range from training to assigning passwords and user IDs. If this isn't done, then all the attention given to security is likely to be compromised because of a lack of consistency in bringing network users onto the network.

The overriding concern that surfaces throughout these events is whether the perception that the network never works is being created. If library staff become convinced that the network is "down" more than it is "up," library administration may have a struggle in convincing staff to make full use of the network. If library staff perceive these events as part of a regularly scheduled maintenance process that can typically be anticipated and worked around, they can maintain their faith in the network.

Staffing

Although not part of the list presented earlier in this chapter, staff affect every item on the list and many others. The importance of training has been discussed in previous chapters but training, by itself, may not be sufficient to ensure that staff will begin to use the local area network. Peer or group pressure may persuade a library staff member that it is better not to use the network, even though he/she may want to, rather than risk antagonizing other library staff. Library administration and the network administrator should realize that some staff will not use the network regardless of the amount of training. Other staff will use the network in certain conditions and not others. There even will be staff who use the network in ways that no one could have anticipated. Understanding the existence of these conditions among the staff is one of the reasons why it is critical for the network administrator to be out among the library staff every day. It is important for the library administration, obviously, to be out there, as well.

If library administration has decided that use of the local area network is important to the continued effective functioning of the library, every effort should be made to remove alternative possibilities from the staff so that they have little choice in terms of using the network. This is important to remember as the effectiveness of workgroups is examined. Since the bulk of a staff member's communication, coordination of work, and sharing of information takes place within the immediate workgroup, attention should be focused on the network alternatives they have and the workgroup consensus that has developed regarding the network. This examination can be an integral part of what should be a regular review, led by library administration, of the manner in which work processes are arranged and the flow of work occurs.

Library administration and network administrators would do well to remember that learning to use a local area network to even a portion of its potential is different from most other activities library staff will have experienced.

> A certain level of LAN usage is needed on a regular basis in order for the user to maintain his willingness and ability to use the system. Local area networks are... 'an intelligent technology' rather than an 'industrial technology.' And because of this, the kind of learning necessary to have LANs used will be different. '...industrial technologies...require a much greater proportion of learning time devoted to training' and rather less to something... described as 'adaptive, ongoing.' 'Adaptive, ongoing' refers to a kind of learning different from training which one acquires over time with the constant use of a specific technology. By using the technology over some period of time, a user begins to see uses of the technology not intially considered. 'Intellectual technologies' require a much greater proportion of time devoted to this 'adaptive, ongoing' type of learning.[1]

What this means in terms of day-to-day activity is that library staff must begin to actually use the network. It means, too, that if the library is large enough to have a staff development and/or personnel librarian, these individuals should be involved in the task of helping to design the training, carry out the training, and then work with staff members on a one-on-one basis to cope with the inevitable adjustments that will be taking place.

Applications

The local area network by itself will not cause any change in the library's organizational structure or effectiveness. The two things that will change these are the application software that is made available over the network and the commitment of the library administration to integrating the network into the library in a seamless manner.

The applications that may have the most immediate potential, if the library has selected them, are electronic mail, calendaring, and scheduling. These three activities in a networked environment can eliminate an enormous level of frustration and wasted effort on the part of the entire library staff. Very quickly these three activities can demonstrate the usefulness of the network. All three depend upon extensive participation by all network users. Library staff cannot sit on the sidelines and expect these services to function well.

Administrative support of these functions can be critical and need involve nothing more than a commitment to distribute memos and announcements; post library calendars; send minutes of meetings; schedule meetings; schedule conference rooms; and schedule equipment. If the only way in which this information or these activities occurs is over the network, staff will quickly internalize the skills needed. Time taken to distribute information to the staff will be reduced, and the ability of each staff member to remain informed should improve. As staff become familiar with these features, they will begin to recognize other opportunities for using these applications that might have been difficult to forecast. Library administration should remember that it is important for them to set the tone in terms of use of the network and use of the equipment, and that means a workstation or PC on the director's desk.

Security

While it may seem contradictory, in the effort to build use of and enthusiasm for the local area network, do not provide too much information to too many staff. The principle of providing staff with sufficient information for them to do their job and no more is easily forgotten as the network administrator struggles to make the network an integral part of the library environment. It is far easier to provide additional information or access rights than it is to take them away from a staff member. Not everyone needs to be a network administrator or supervisor.

Periodically, the network administrator should review not only network performance with the senior library administration, but the effectiveness of security policies and procedures. If the network is being compromised by staff or individuals outside the library, library administration must be informed as quickly as possible and steps must be taken to remedy the situation. This is another instance in which library administration must publicly demonstrate its commitment to making the network succeed.

One of the areas in which the network administrator should be vigilant is experimentation. Inevitably, there will be individuals among the library staff who want to try something different on the network. They may know just enough to be dangerous in terms of their ability to proceed without the aid, support, and assistance of the network administrator. Even before the network becomes operational, library staff should be indoctrinated to the idea that while there is a receptiveness to developing new ways to use the network, there is also a set procedure that must be followed. If the procedures aren't used, library administration must be prepared to take disciplinary action if circumstances warrant.

As the network settles into its routine operation, the network administrator should be sensitive to the following types of intrusion that might take place on the network.

'Passive monitoring,' or secretly reading network information, is one of the most common methods of network abuse. It allows individuals to read valuable information without making any detectable changes to the information on the network. Another method 'spying,' allows an individual to pick up passwords that can be used for further abuse, or simply to pick up information not accessible in other ways. 'Spoofing' occurs when someone attaches to a network and assumes the identity and characteristics of a valid user. Once on the network, the individual can do things the valid user can do, including read and change information, send messages, and change the way the other computers work, such as setting up a new identity for later use. Even if someone is unable to simulate completely an authorized user or computer, he or she can disrupt a computer's operation by recording and playing back network activity.[2]

Never assume that just because a library is involved, there is not an individual out there waiting to create mischief in the library local area network. It will happen, someday, some way.

Complacency can occur in the form of forgetting the network equipment room if the network seems to be functioning correctly. Spend some time in the network equipment room every day checking the monitors on the servers. NOVELL's software will alert the system administrator to daily tasks that should be reviewed. For example, if an error checking method of three tries to correctly type in a user's password has been installed, the server software will alert the administrator to those instances when an individual has been locked out or has typed his/her password incorrectly four successive times. This might mean one of several things, but it is important to follow up immediately. First, it is possible the network user forgot his/her password. Second, perhaps, a staff member is trying to use someone else's password with their permission and has forgotten the password. Third, it may be the user's typing skill is minimal. Calling the user that has been locked out to determine if they are having a problem will demonstrate that there is ongoing monitoring of network activity and that someone is committed to protecting their files.

Experience has demonstrated that it is worthwhile for the systems administrator to be logged into all the servers at all times. There are two reasons for this. First, the administrator can be aware of any problems that may happen during the work day. If a server goes down, NOVELL software will alert all the users on the network that the server is down. Second, network users have the capability to communicate directly and easily with the network administrator. If it is not possible or practical to have the network administrator logged in at all times, then it may be appropriate for all of the local area networks to have a terminal close to the network administrator for quick access to evaluate problems.

7
LAN Expansion

There seems to be general acceptance of the premise that local area networks are bound to grow. As soon as they are installed, and many times before they are operating, staff begin to petition for additional nodes and branches to be added to the network. Network administrators and library administration must remember that network growth should be addressed in an orderly planned fashion, a condition that has not always characterized libraries. Growth that occurs in a spontaneous unplanned manner will result in unnecessary expenditures for equipment that is not needed, applications that cannot be used, and a network that may become dysfunctional. Libraries cannot afford these types of errors.

Although it may seem unfair to those library staff who aren't in the first wave of network implementation, a measured orderly expansion of the local area network is better for everyone. If the proper planning and design were done at the beginning of the project and the staff kept informed, there should be some level of understanding among staff on this issue. Local area networks must operate efficiently and successfully. The loss of irreplaceable data files and the confidence of library staff should not be permitted to happen.

As the design and selection process for the local area network began, library personnel should have approached the task by overestimating the "opening day" requirements for the network. It is far safer to have an excess of capacity initially than to begin using the network and immediately have staff complain that it is inadequate for their needs. It is not necessary that every projected workstation or PC be tied into the network on the first day, but plans should have been made to add those pieces of equipment and thought put into where they could be installed. In the same vein, if some thought has gone into the manner in which the network might be expanded through branching or the creation of linkages to additional local area networks, a substantial amount of second-guessing can be avoided later on.

Growth and expansion in the local area network must be based upon clearly justified need. The mere fact that an individual or workgroup wants a particular piece of equipment, additional workstations, or PCs added is not sufficient for the library administration to approve the expenditure. The network administrator should expect to demonstrate through quanitifiable data, not just anecdotal evidence, that there is demand that justifies the use of scarce resources for the network. While network expenditures should be justified, library administration must integrate network support into the regular budgetary processes for the library. Network funding should not be based on a series of one-time, non-recurring expenditures that flow from the largess of some parent funding agency.

The nature of the computer industry makes long-range planning, such as five years or more, unrealistic. It is reasonable for network administrators and library administrators to use a planning window of two years for local area networking, recognizing that the plan is undergoing almost continuous revision. There seems to be evidence that use of the typical local area network will increase between 30 percent and 50 percent in the first year. If this evidence is accurate, it may be very difficult to overestimate the "opening day" projections of the need for a local area network. The assumption should be that the local area network will be successful, probably wildly so, and plan accordingly. A guiding consideration should be to attempt to match the growth or expansion of the network to the growth in or expansion of skills among the library staff. The ideal situation would be a network that expands in response to the increasing sophistication of the staff in addition to including new groups of staff as users.

As network growth is projected, the network administrator must keep in mind that there are at least two different life cycles represented. "The physical network should have a life cycle of over 10 years, whereas the message network may have a life cycle of less than five years."[1] Whether a particular library's network will fall within these boundaries will be determined by a variety of factors, many of which the library has no control over.

Regardless of the life cycle of various aspects of the network, the demand for growth, or the advent of new networking technology, justification has to be expected before expansion is funded. The network administrator must have something better than anecdotal evidence. Claiming that staff are having to wait for their work to be processed or output printed isn't sufficient. If the network administrator can provide statistics that demonstrate that staff are having to wait an hour to have material printed, a request for additional printing equipment can be justified more easily. Network operating software should offer the capability for the network administrator to collect a substantial amount of this type of data. Other software packages and pieces of equipment can augment this data collection as well. These software applications have evolved in the last year and many more of them will be available in the next few years. Collecting data will enable the network administrator to begin to do projections on the growth of parts of the network and, perhaps, anticipate where bottlenecks will begin to develop. If forecasting can be done, a great deal of unnecessary frustration can be removed from the daily work routines of library staff.

As library staff increase their use of the network and their level of sophistication regarding the network, higher speed equipment will inevitably be added to the network. Unless the bandwidth of the network expands over time, a bottleneck in the network's capacity to handle the increased traffic may develop. Similarly, the servers on a network should have network adapters added that permit them to accommodate the higher-speed workstations. A great deal of attention is given to adding the fastest possible PCs or workstations to the network, but the capacity of the connectors, bridges, routers, gateways, and servers to handle the faster speed is often forgotten. If the capacity of these parts of the network is not increased, the flow of traffic on the network will remain the same or seem even slower than before.

An aspect of network growth that is often ignored is the increase in network applications that are made available to library staff. Before a new application is loaded on the network, some analysis should be done to determine the impact on the performance of the network. As more and more shared applications are placed on the network, the potential for degradation in transmission speed increases. Monitoring network performance is a must.

Regardless of the topology chosen for the library's network, the time may come when, instead of adding to the network, library administration should consider the creation of new local area networks. Rather than rerouting the cabling of the existing network, it may be simpler to add a new network, thus avoiding the downtime that would have resulted while the rerouting was taking place. Smaller, limited local area networks that are bridged or routed make trouble-shooting much easier since small portions of the organization can be taken out of the totally networked environment.

Expansion of the local area network may mean connecting to the parent organization's network regardless of whether that organization is a municipality, corporation, or educational institution. It probably is appropriate to assume that this need will surface at some time, even if it seems remote when network planning is beginning. If projections are made for this from the very start, it may be possible to avoid problems related to hardware or software incompatibility. It is possible that certain pieces of expensive equipment such as gateways might be avoided.

Most library local area networks are installed to facilitate the work of library staff providing access to electronic mail, word processing, calendaring, scheduling, spreadsheets, and database software. Very quickly a bewildering assortment of other features and equipment are identified as being desirable for the library's network. Scanning equipment and the necessary OCR software, facsimile boards, modems, CD-ROM equipment and supporting software, animation programs, and video resources beckon as attractive and, possibly, necessary additions to the network. Each of these presents unique challenges and opportunities to the growth of the local area network. Considerable caution should be excercised when analyzing the claims of vendors offering these products to network users.

Compact disc products have focused the attention of libraries on the potential of networking in a way that nothing else has. The importance of CD-ROM technology to the information community seems undisputed but the implications for library local area networking are less understood. There is still a considerable amount of work to be done to make CD-ROM networking an easy, painless experience for libraries. Some of the frustrations relate to the technical difficulties surrounding the compatibility of various drivers, the absence of any standards (although there seem to be some de facto standards), the use of SCSI interfaces, and the newness of high-speed 386 and 486 equipment. Non-technical issues that are just as important involve vendor licensing of CD-ROM products for network use, the question of who owns the product, and differential pricing of paper and disc products. It will still be some time before these issues are resolved.

Remote network access is an issue that each library will have to settle on its own. Any network user with the appropriate rights and software can use all of the functions of the network. This has tremendous potential for two groups of network users. First, library staff, properly equipped, could access their own files on the network from their home or other remote locations. This could prove to be invaluable. Second, library patrons who have access to a personal computer/terminal and modem could access public files on the library's local area network. While security issues can never be forgotten, the prospect of being able to mount new locally important databases reflecting library and community resources is very attractive.

While there is software such as Carbon Copy that will allow a remote user to call a network and with an appropriate password become a local user, there is the reality that high-speed modems are needed to make this practical. This means the library must anticipate the need for a modem server that can respond to calls coming in at a variety of speeds to the network. The most worrisome issue in this arena is the question of training for the potential users who might want this type of access.

As local area networks have developed, a variety of third-party software has been offered to network users. Some of this software is very good and other packages are less satisfactory. Each library will have to be the judge of whether a package meets the library's expectations. Three applications from Fresh Technology are offered as examples of the types of software available in the marketplace.

The first is LAN ASSIST. This program permits a network administrator to help others on the network without having to leave her/his office. The administrator is able to view the user's screen on her/his screen and take control of the functioning of the remote machine. This can be a tremendous aid in solving a user's problems.

The second is PRINT ASSIST. This is a temporary stay resident (TSR) program that permits a network user to use printers that are neither attached to the person's workstation or to the server. The result is improved sharing of peripherals. High-quality printers can be placed in central locations and all local users can route their printing to that device. Savings can result from a reduction in the number of printers that must be purchased and the time to route materials to be printed. It is possible that the need for this type of application may be minimized by newer versions of network software, such as NOVELL Netware 386 with its remote printing feature.

A third product is MAP ASSIST, another TSR program. This application permits a person working at one workstation to use another workstation as if it were the local one. The result is that with proper installation a person at one workstation could use the hard disks at another workstation as if they were located on the first unit. The uses for this product are fairly dramatic. Sharing high-speed modems, tape back-up units, fax boards, scanners, and CD-ROMs easily come to mind as items to be shared.

Whether these specific products would work in a specific library must depend upon the analysis of the network administrator. Regardless of the software application being considered, there is usually a wide selection to choose from. Careful review and evaluation must be the standard in determining what will be best for each library.

As care should have been exercised in installing and operating the network, so should care characterize the expansion of the local area network. Be certain that a significant portion of the existing capacity of the network is being used before approving expansion. Require evidence of the need before committing to the expenditures for growth. Additionally, be absolutely certain that the options available in the marketplace have been fully explored and that staff have the capacity to handle the expansion that is being sought.

The literature of local area networking suggests that the effect a local area network can have on an organization is bound to be successful. The organization that adopts local area networking, if done correctly, will see its productivity increase dramatically, its employees become more effective in their work, and its standing in its community improve proportionately.

However, there are instances where local area networking has not been the answer to all an organization's needs. While there are not many instances where a local area network has been taken out once it is installed, local area network failure is more often characterized by the fact that expectations are not met and work continues to be accomplished in the same old manner. When this happens, management and staff, in a library or some other organization, must look within themselves for the real reasons for the lack of achievement. The lack of success is not the fault of the local area network, it is the failure of people to capitalize upon opportunities waiting for them. The approach to successful local area networking requires that same attention to detail and hard work that accompanies any other endeavor.

Throughout this book the need for thorough planning and preparation is mentioned repeatedly. Unless library personnel take the time to plan, design, install, and implement a local area network that reflects the needs of the library, its staff, and clientele, the local area network will not meet expectations. Equally as important is the need for library managers to be prepared for a substantial commitment of their time to effecting the successful adoption of a local area network. While other library staff may perform the actual installation, library administration must be in the forefront of utilizing the local area network.

Effective utilization of a local area network will be increasingly important for at least two reasons in the years ahead. First, there will continue to be great pressure to do more with less. The result will be a search for ways to capitalize on the continued development of electronic technologies that have implications for the transfer of information. Second, electronic networks at the regional, state, national, and international level will come to dominate our lives as librarians in the balance of this century and the first years of the next millenium as the cost of information continues to grow and the need to share increases. Local area networking will provide the framework within which the individual library will make its connection to the larger networked world.

Appendices

The appendices that follow are an assortment of checklists the authors have found in their reading and discussions involving local area networking or developed as they worked through the evolution of the library networks they have installed. Once again, these lists should not be considered as the "final word" and should be adapted and modified to suit the circumstances of each reader and library. The most important contribution any of these checklists can make is to trigger the reader's own review of the steps that must be taken during a particular phase of networking. If these checklists can facilitate a library's entry into local area networking then their purpose will have been fulfilled.

Appendix A: The Steps to Effective LAN Management

The following outline is drafted from Cheryl C. Currid's, "Planning, Designing and Staffing LANs." *Networking Management* 8, no.3 (March 1990), 62.

1. Planning
   a. End-users must be drivers of activity.
   b. Central and consistent vision.
   c. Electronic links to and from desktop.
   d. Electronic links to outside world.
2. Staffing
   a. Well-qualified people are hard to find.
   b. Staff will be involved in a variety of activities.
   c. Small, centrally located group of administrators.
   d. Shared responsibilities for LAN administration.
   e. Develop "extended family" of outside talent.
3. LAN Architecture
   a. Consistent approach to installation of application software.
   b. Generic software for basic applications.
   c. Allow for installation of custom software applications.
4. Maintenance Budgeting
   a. Adequately funded budget for LAN maintenance.
   b. Determine cost of spare or replacement hardware.
   c. Plan for network operating system and application upgrades.
5. Effective LAN Management
   a. The right tools.
   b. The right team.
   c. The right funding.

As a library staff and administration consider whether local area networking is appropriate for their library, this checklist of steps may provide a reasonable outline of the realities and challenges that must be addressed. The categories of planning, staffing, and budgeting should be analyzed carefully in deciding whether or not to embark on a local area networking project. Proper planning will require a discipline that many libraries will find difficult to adhere to and complete. Partial planning for local area networking may be worse than no planning at all and will certainly establish a recipe for problems if not disaster at a later date.

Staffing of new projects is often taken for granted especially by the library's parent organization. Libraries have done an exceptional job of absorbing the personnel demands of previous new endeavors. If not properly staffed with skilled personnel, local area networking will bring misery and recrimination to the library staff. Do not expect existing library staff to absorb the responsibilities for local area networking into their present assignments. Effective local area networking will require the full-time commitment of one, and perhaps more, library staff members. Library administration should anticipate that networking staff will be in constant turmoil because of turnover as individuals are hired away to better paying and more attractive positions, sometimes by the parent organization.

Budgeting may be the weakest link in local area networking for libraries, even if the rest of their preparations are accomplished effectively. An ongoing commitment of budget resources will be required. The inevitable growth of local area networks as additional staff are placed on the network, additional equipment is needed, and new applications are identified, will place an insatiable demand for increased funding. Unless the library's budget is growing annually, those funds will have to be taken from other activities. The implications of those future decisions need to be accepted by all library staff before local area networking begins.

Appendix B: Applications Software Selection Considerations

The following outline is drafted from Rowland Archer's, *The Practical Guide to Local Area Networks.* (Berkeley, Calif.: Osborne McGraw-Hill, 1986): 57.

1. Business
   a. Problems to solve.
   b. Improvements sought.
   c. Conversion from existing system.
   d. Financial resources to purchase system.
2. People
   a. End-user computer sophistication.
   b. End-user need and ability to modify applications.
   c. In-house or outside custom programming availability.
   d. Network management responsibility.
3. Software
   a. Applicability to problems at hand.
   b. User interface suitability.
   c. Integration with other applications.
   d. Shared database access across network.
   e. Custom programming requirement.
   f. Ability and need to modify source code.

Appendix C: Checklist for Trial Network Evaluation

The following outline is drafted from Rowland Archer's, *The Practical Guide to Local Area Networks.* (Berkeley, Calif.: Osborne McGraw-Hill, 1986): 55.

I. Disk Storage
  A. Performance
    1. Responsiveness (delay from request to action).
    2. Transfer speed (time to load and save files).
    3. Consistency (variations in performance).
  B. File Placement
    1. Convenience (ease of locating and accessing).
    2. Usability (able to access disk from all applications).
II. Print Service
  A. Performance
    1. Usability (print from all applications).
    2. Spooling (time workstation is tied up while printing).
  B. Job Management
    1. Sharing (distribution of printers to users).
    2. Separating (distinguishing different users' printouts).
    3. Forms (need to change print forms often).
III. Systems Software
  A. Operating environment
    1. Understanding (quality of training).
    2. Ease of use (ease of doing necessary tasks).
    3. Functionality (can do all necessary tasks).
    4. Reliability (as compared to single-user PC).
  B. Security
    1. Functionality (keeps unwarranted users out).
    2. Convenience (not cumbersome to authorized users).

IV. Applications Software
    A. Personal programs
        1. Usability (can use programs on network as desired).
        2. Licensing (do users understand license issues).
    B. Multi-user network applications
        1. Sharing (any problems with concurrent data access).
        2. Functionality (does intended job).

As the local area network administrator and appropriate library staff proceed with the investigation of possible local area network systems, some type of evaluation framework is indispensable to ensure that the assessment is consistent across all products. This list, while certainly not exhaustive, can serve as the basis for developing a library's specific list of evaluative criteria.

It may be appropriate to develop two lists. The first can be used as visits are made to sites that are already functioning with a local area network and prospective vendors to confirm the strengths and weaknesses of the various products that will be seen. The second list should be a much longer one that weighs the various features that are sought in the local area network that will be installed in the library. This list can be used to evaluate the finalists that are being considered for a library's local area network. It can also serve as the basis for developing the checklist of conditions that must be met before the final sign-off occurs after the network has been installed.

Appendix D: Network Checkup List

The following outline is drafted from Peter Stephenson, David Buerger, and Raphael Needleman's, "Managing Your LAN: A Balance of Many Skills." *Infoworld* 11, no.6, Target Edition no.3, p. S3.

1. Cable
    a. Look for snags or twists.
    b. Did anybody add equipment without telling you?
2. Printers
    a. Check print servers, spoolers, and print queues.
    b. Check supplies, ribbons, toner, paper.
    c. Is there printout waiting to be distributed?
3. Servers
    a. Are the error rate and response time acceptable?
    b. Are you running low on disk space?
4. Software
    a. Is it working as expected?
    b. Are users requesting more or different software?
    c. Have there been bug reports?
5. Files
    a. Are there old files you can delete (backup, temporary, scratch)?
6. Automatic network logs
    a. Look for unusual error counts and potential security breaches.
7. Supplies
    a. Do you have sufficient spare parts and cables?
8. Backup
    a. Perform data backup.
    b. Make sure media are within useful life.
    c. Check UPSs.
9. Paperwork
    a. Update cabling maps, equipment inventory, maintenance records, network diary.

10. People
    a. Check your e-mail.
    b. Talk to network users.

As the local area network becomes functional, a daily routine for monitoring network performance and behavior should be established. This list provides some of the items that a local area network administrator may want to make part of the local routine. The important consideration to remember is that these activities become part of the preventive maintenance schedule in the sense that they may permit the network administrator to anticipate problems while they are in their infancy. Incipient problems that can be identified before they become interruptions in the smooth functioning of the network are much more easily addressed.

The goal of the local area network administrator should be to have the network operating so effectively that it becomes part of the invisible background of the library. When library staff no longer think of or consider the local area network to be a unique factor in the library environment, then it can become an integral facet of the library infrastructure. Accomplishing this condition is directly dependent upon the ability to keep the network functioning without interrupting the work routines of the library staff. This presumes that potential problems will be identified and diagnosed long before they become problems and that a schedule for preventive maintenance will be established that minimizes interference with the daily job routines of library staff.

Appendix E: Management Checklist

The following outline is a checklist which will aid in the assessment of whether or not local area networking is appropriate for an individual library.

    I. Evaluate whether or not a local area network will be beneficial to the organization.
    II. Will benefits of the LAN outweigh its costs?
    III. Itemize and assign value to all costs.
    IV. If you decide a network is appropriate, then:
        A. Select and appoint a network administrator.
            1. Provide a job description.
            2. To whom does the network administrator reports?
            3. Where in the organization do network activities belong or report to?
                a. the library automation or system's unit.
                b. an associate or assistant director.
                c. the director.
        B. Develop budget for network project. Must be an on-going realistic budget that considers as a minimum the following cost centers:
            1. Hardware
            2. Software
            3. Training
            4. Maintenance
                a. repair
                b. replacement
            5. Evolution or growth in the network
            6. Installation and renovation
            7. Consumables
                a. disks
                b. paper
                c. printer ribbon/toner

      C. Provide network administrator with sufficient authority to achieve successful implementation of network.

      D. Develop a system that will provide all staff with a continuous flow of information about how the LAN project is progressing.

      E. Identify and select support people who will become the local experts for each of the software application packages.

          1. Modify job descriptions to reflect new assignments.

      F. Provide adequate training for all staff who will be working with the network and the applications software.

          1. Need to determine whether there is the capacity for in-house training or should external trainers be used.

          2. Training will have to be structured so it is useful to staff with widely varying interests and skills.

          3. Need to be sensitive to training supervisory and administrative staff in a manner that is non-threatening to them.

   V. Regardless of what your decision about a network is, maintain a complete, fully documented record of all decisions and the material used to arrive at the decisions.

   VI. Develop a program which will ensure that top management in the library or the institution is kept informed of the progress you are making.

Library administration can be left "holding the bag" in a local area networking project if they do not have a clear understanding of what their own and other staff responsibilities should be. In the final analysis, the library director is the individual who must make the basic decision about whether or not local area networking makes sense at a particular time and place for the library. There may be enthusiastic pressure from library staff to join in the networked world that all other libraries seem to be pursuing. No one wants to be left out or come late to the table. There may be substantial pressure from a parent organization to join in the enterprise-wide networking effort. Accountability rests with the library administration for the decision and this checklist can provide a partial road map for that individual seeking a solution.

Careful analysis, clear delineation of benefits and liabilities are needed in order to achieve a dispassionate assessment of whether or not local area networking is appropriate for a library. The total cost of the project, not just the one-time costs but the complete life cycle costs of local area networking need to be identified and quantified. Any attempt to forecast the budgetary future of a library is filled with pitfalls but that task must be undertaken. Conscious choices will have to be identified and communicated to library staff so they understand the options that are being considered.

While it is natural to focus attention on the budgetary, equipment, and physical plant implications of local area networking, there is another more subtle aspect of networking that the library director must evaluate. Does the library staff have the capacity to work through the changes in work relationships and organizational structure that may flow from a successful local area network installation? If it is concluded that the staff is not ready for local area networking, then it should be delayed and the groundwork done to prepare them for it.

Appendix F: Hardware Checklist

The following outline was developed to serve as an inventory checklist to evaluate equipment needed as well as equipment already existing for use in a local area network.

- A. Server
    1. Central
    2. Decentralized
    3. Print
    4. Modem
- B. Workstations
    1. Diskless
- C. Modems
- D. Network printers
    1. Dot matrix
    2. Laser
    3. Daisy wheel
- E. UPS
- F. Surge protectors
- G. Network Interface Cards
- H. Cable
    1. Twisted pair
        a. unshielded
        b. shielded
    2. coaxial
    3. fiber optic
- I. Backup systems
    1. Tape back up
    2. Disk mirroring
- J. Spare parts/replacement inventory
    1. Identify replacement schedules for all equipment associated with the network.
- K. Take an inventory of all equipment complete with registration numbers. Be certain to keep this up to date, especially when new equipment is received.

The hardware checklist can serve several purposes. The first is as a framework for taking inventory of existing equipment that might be useful in a local area network. This will help library administration evaluate the investment that already is in place. Second, the checklist can be used to identify the types and quantities of equipment that will be needed to install the local area network initially, and then types of and quantities of equipment that may be needed at certain milestones later. Finally, the checklist can provide the basis for a working inventory of equipment assigned to the local area network as the installation takes place.

The major undertaking will be to keep the inventory up to date with proper recording of serial numbers, repair history for each piece of equipment, and modifications that have been made. There is a natural tendency to put off these activities in the press of trying to solve the crises that seem to occur at the wrong time. Library administration and the network administrator must have the same commitment to making certain this task is kept up to date. To ensure this happens, the library administration may have to establish a policy that all computing-related purchase requests have to pass through the network administrator's hands for review. Further, all computer-related equipment as it is received will have to be cleared by the administrator to ensure the recording of serial numbers, the filing of registration forms, and to avoid incompatibility problems by checking the setup of equipment.

Appendix G: Software Checklist

The following outline was designed to aid in the decision of which software to choose. It cannot be overemphasized that backup copies of all software including the operating system software should be made before beginning the installation of any software.

A. Network operating system
B. Value added processes (VAP)
    1. MAC VAP
C. Special network software
    1. LAN Assist
    2. MAP Assist
    3. Print Assist
    4. Sparkle (Modem sharing)
    5. Site Lock (limits the number of concurrent users of a software application)
    6. Carbon Copy (remote access software)

It is recommended that before any application software is loaded on the network a decision be made to standardize on specific brands and versions of software.

D. Application software
    1. Will user success with the network be improved by use of a shell application?
    2. Evaluate present software to determine whether or not site licenses are held?
        a. Number of users permitted to access software applications.
        b. Is the software networkable?
    3. Is a network site license available for the software?
    4. Who will use each of the software applications to be loaded?
    5. What rights will each user have to each software

application?
a. Read, Read/Write?
b. Which directories does each user have access to?
E. Be certain that all software registration forms are completed and turned in.
F. Take an inventory of all software complete with registration numbers. Be certain to keep this up to date, especially when new releases or updates are received.
G. Have you identified individuals who will become the specialists for the different software applications adopted by the organization?
1. These people should become the interface for the staff and the software firm when problems arise.
H. Make certain that backups are made of all software including the network software.

The natural focus of attention in local area networking is the network operating software and the necessary hardware to install the network. In fact, the more serious problems may arise as the question of applications software arises. Too often this topic is not addressed during the planning for local area networking. Unfortunately, if it is not raised in the planning there can be substantial disappointment later on.

Clearly, one of the most important issues to resolve is whether there will be a limited number of software applications allowed on the network and, therefore, supported by the network administrator. Allowing an unrestricted number of software applications on a local area network seems to be an invitation to disaster considering the problems that exist with viruses and similar products. There may be compatibility problems between different applications that are not apparent in the stand-alone personal computing environment. Finally, there is a limit to the diversity of software that a network administrator can be expected to support and a limit to the number of applications for which a library can afford to provide training opportunities.

The procedures in place for hardware purchases and installation should be established for software applications. The local area network administrator should approve all purchases and receive all software coming into the library so it can be registered and checked before being loaded onto the network. This is particularly important when the software or data are being received from a source other than an established vendor.

Appendix H: Installation Checklist

The following outline was created to aid in the planning, installation, and documentation of a newly developed local area network.

A. Begin a diary of every activity engaged in related to the implementation of the network.

B. Develop a map or layout of all cabling installed in hooking the equipment onto the network. Remember the footage it takes to come down the wall and then go back up.

C. Create an inventory of the equipment that will be located at each workstation site, the software applications that each user will have available to them, and the security level assigned to them.

D. Develop a plan for order in which equipment and cable will be installed and follow it strictly.

E. Run all cables to spaces where workstations, server(s), and peripherals will be located. Allow for some movement of the cables inside the offices but do not spool 20-30 feet in a location. No connections are attached at this time.

F. Set up the server and one workstation to create a mini-network. Make certain it works before proceeding.

G. Install network interface cards in all machines scheduled to be hooked up initially.

H. Once the server is functioning in the mini-network environment, install all application software and make certain it works in the test environment.

I. Work installing one workstation at a time, verifying all connections are functioning.

J. Set up network security for each user using the information collected in step C, above.

K. Set up network shells for each user using the information collected in step C, above.

L. Establish a naming formula for assigning network names to all users.

M. Begin preliminary instruction with users on what the network is, how to use it, how it differs from a stand-alone PC. Permit users to ask all the questions they want about the network.

N. Install and test all peripherals, including printers, modems, backup systems, etc.

O. Begin a regular schedule of backups on the network.

P. Identify an off-site location for backup tapes of the network's files.

Q. Identify a secure location for housing the network server and other centrally held equipment that is readily accessible to the network administrator and/or supervisor.

Successfully completing the installation of a local area network is largely a matter of identifying the steps that must be taken and then establishing a routine that encompasses all of them. Although most people tend to ignore the fundamental need for documentation, this step ought to precede all other steps in the installation process. Dedication to documentation may be the best indicator of whether or not the library administration, network administrator, and library staff are committed to doing local area networking right.

Effective local area network installation is analogous to building a brick wall. Each component of the network needs to be installed and tested before moving onto the next part of the system. Begin the network installation with the smallest possible configuration, the server and one or two workstations. Install them, test them and make certain they are operating successfully before adding other workstations or peripherals.

Daily or weekly review sessions between the individuals directly involved in network installation and library administration will provide the opportunity for a "reality check" of the process and what has been accomplished. If there are problems, they should be acknowledged and identified as quickly as possible. It is important that installation be completed in a timely manner, but it is critical that installation be done correctly the first time.

Appendix I: Training Checklist

The following outline was developed to draw attention to the importance of training and the necessary preparations to take in order to have a successful local area network.

    A. Once a network administrator has been appointed, determine the training that person is to receive.

    B. Determine whether in-house training or external trainers will be used to train the staff.

    C. Determine the priority in which staff should be trained and the current levels of computer and/or networking skills and knowledge of the staff.

    D. Set up a training room where individuals can be instructed without distraction.

    E. Determine whether or not the supervisory and management personnel should have separate or individual training sessions.

    F. Determine whether staff understand the role of passwords and the importance of network security.

    G. Determine the level of training and expertise required of all application software specialists.

    H. Establish a schedule for training in the various application software packages.

    I. Try to establish a non-threatening learning environment in which staff have an opportunity to learn at their own pace and ask all the questions they need to.

    J. Make certain that each staff member has had an opportunity to complete any tutorial that may be supplied by the vendors.

    K. For software applications determine if there are learning packages available that can enhance the opportunity for staff to build their expertise with an application.

    L. If external training programs are considered, be certain to evaluate them in terms of their applicability to your local situation.

M. Be prepared to have to retrain individuals unless you can create
an environment in which they use the network every day.

Training may turn out to be the largest network cost for which a library
has to budget. The problem is that training is often a hidden cost and,
certainly, a soft cost. Training or staff development has traditionally
received lip service in most libraries but little of real substance has typically
been achieved. Local area networking focuses the attention of the entire
library staff on the importance of proper training. If effective, timely
training is not provided, the local area network will not be effective.

The task of training library staff to use the local area network will never
be completed because of the turnover in staff. Similarly, it will never be
completed because, inevitably, new applications or features will be added to
the network. The challenge for most libraries will be to integrate the need
for training into the rest of the demands on staff.

Appendix J: Budget Checklist

The following outline was designed to help the library prepare for the costs of a local area network and begin the necessary budgeting.

    I. What are the sources of funds that will be available to support networking?
        A. One-time non-recurring funds
            1. Appropriated funds
            2. Gift funds
            3. Grant funds
        B. Continuing or base budget funds
            1. Special continuing appropriation
            2. Existing automation budget
   II. Develop budget for network project. Must be an ongoing realistic budget that considers as a minimum the following cost centers:
        A. Hardware
            1. Cable
            2. Workstations
            3. Server
            4. Peripherals
                a. Printers
                b. Modems
                c. Telefacsimile
                d. CD-ROM
                e. UPSs *Uninterruptable Power Sup[ply]*
        B. Software
            1. Network
            2. Applications
        C. Training
            1. Specialized training for LAN administrator
            2. General staff training
        D. Maintenance
            1. Repair

        2. Replacement
   E. Evolution of or growth in the network
   F. Installation and renovation
   G. Consumables
        1. Disks
        2. Paper
        3. Printer ribbon/toner
   H. Travel
        1. Identify those items which should be bid and those which are incidental expense items

One of the greatest dangers of local area networking is the tendency to under budget for the activity. There is a natural tendency to focus on the obvious "hard" costs and overlook both the "soft" and "hidden" costs that are associated with local area networking. Unless all costs are clearly identified, it is conceivable that a local area network could be only partially installed while the library had exhausted its available funds.

This budget checklist is not exhaustive but it can provide the trigger to identify those costs, both general and unique, that apply to a particular library and, at the same time, identify both the one-time and recurring costs that must be anticipated. Although it may be a new concept to the library administration, it is wise to identify the life cycle costs of the local area network to be certain that the project is one the library can truly afford.

Notes

Chapter 1

1. James S. Fritz, Charles F. Kaldenbach, and Louis M. Progar, *Local Area Networks: Selection Guidelines* (Englewood Cliffs, N.J.: Prentice-Hall, Inc., 1985), 4.

2. Michael Kleeman et al., *PC LAN Primer* (Indianapolis, Ind.: Howard W. Sams & Co., 1987), xi.

3. Raphael Needleman, "Server-Based and Peer-to-Peer LAN Designs," *InfoWorld* 11, no. 46, Target Edition no. 36 (November 13, 1989): S23.

4. "NICs: The Nerves of a LAN," *LAN Times* (April 1988): 58.

5. Brendan Tangney and Donal O'Mahony, *Local Area Networks and their Applications* (Englewood Cliffs, N.J.: Prentice-Hall, Inc., 1988), 18-20.

6. Ibid., 20-21.

7. James Harry Green, *Local Area Networks: A User's Guide for Business Professionals* (Glenview, Ill.: Scott, Foresman and Company, 1985), 31.

8. Rowland Archer, *The Practical Guide to Local Area Networks* (Berkeley, Calif.: Osborne, McGraw-Hill, 1986), 43.

9. Brett Glass, "Netbios: The Most Misunderstood LAN Interface," *InfoWorld* 12, no. 16, Target Edition no. 13 (April 16, 1990): S15.

Chapter 2

1. Uyless Black, *Computer Networks: Protocals, Standards, and Interfaces* (Englewood Cliffs, N.J.: Prentice-Hall, Inc., 1987), 131.

2. Ibid., 132.

3. Mark Stephens, "Wired: How PC Networks are Changing the Way We Work," *InfoWorld* 11 (March 27, 1989): 41.

Chapter 3

1. William Stallings, *Local Networks: An Introduction* (New York: Macmillan Publishing Company, 1984), 319.

2. Martin A. W. Nemsow, *Keeping the Link: Ethernet Installation and Management* (New York: McGraw-Hill, 1988), 288.

3. Ibid., 288.

4. Stallings, *Local Networks*, 4.

5. Michael F. Hordeski, *Microcomputer LANs: Network Design and Implementation.* (Blue Ridge Summit, Penn.: TAB Professional and Reference Books, 1987), 226-227.

6. Green, *Local Area Networks*, 192.

7. Archer, *The Practical Guide*, 31.

8. Marlyn Kemper, *Networking: Choosing a LAN Path to Interconnection* (Metuchen, N.J.: Scarecrow Press, 1987), 195.

9. Fritz, Kaldenbach, and Progar, *Local Area Networks*, 57.

10. Green, *Local Area Networks*, 36-37.

Chapter 4

1. Green, *Local Area Networks*, 217.

2. Bill Hancock, *Designing and Implementing Ethernet Networks* (Wellesley, Mass.: QED Information Sciences, Inc., 1988), 87-88.

3. Michael Durr and Mark Gibbs, *Networking Personal Computers* (Carmel, Ind.: Cue Corporation, 1989), 307.

4. Archer, *The Practical Guide*, 80.

5. Tom Henderson, "Tips for Network Installers," *Lan Times* (December, 1987): 20.

6. Archer, *The Practical Guide*, 81.

7. Hancock, *Ethernet Networks*, 96-97.

Chapter 5

1. Stephen A. Caswell, "The New Mail," *InfoWorld* 11, no. 39, Target Edition no. 30 (September 25, 1989): S1. Quoted material from Electronic Mail Association.

2. Mike Hurwicz, "Securing the LAN," *LAN Times* (August 1987): 35.

Chapter 6

1. V. E. Cheong and R. A. Hirscheim, Local Area Networks: *Issues, Products, and Developments* (Chichester, England: John Wiley & Sons, 1983), 129.

2. Larry Allen-Tonar, "Networked Computers Attract Security Problems, Abuse," *Networking Management* 7, no. 12 (December 1989): 48.

Chapter 7

1. Fritz, Kaldenbach, and Progar, *Local Area Networks*, 37.

Glossary

The following list of terms has been assembled from a number of publications we have used to build our knowledge of local area networks. Those publications are listed at the conclusion of this glossary.

ADAPTER: An adapter is a device utilized to interface a data terminal to a channel and carry out data rate and code conversion enabling the terminal to be compatible with the required communications standards.

ADDRESS: A combination of numbers or other characters that identify a given local area network node. Addresses are used to indicate nodes for which information transmitted over the network is intended.

ALTERNATE PATH ROUTING: In a network, an alternate path routing deals with the selection of an access path other than the normal or basic access path. An alternate path is usually selected because an intervening transmission link or node is heavily overloaded.

ANALOG: Analog is a representation of a phenomenon in another form such as the representation of voice sounds as electrical audio signals.

ANALOG TRANSMISSION: Analog transmission refers to transmission of a continuously variable signal as opposed to a discretely variable signal.

APPC: Advanced Program-to-Program communications; IBM protocol that allows peer-to-peer communications.

APPLICATIONS LAYER: Seventh level of OSI Reference Model; defines the interface of application software with the network's operating system.

ARCHITECTURE: The architecture of a system refers to its design and the way in which the constituent parts interrelate.

ARCNET: Attached Resources Computing Network; popular network architecture that uses the token-passing bus protocol.

ASYNCHRONOUS: Not synchronized. Can be sent or received when participants choose, not at fixed intervals.

ASYNCHRONOUS TRANSMISSION: Data transmission method where characters are sent one bit at a time. Extra bits are added to the beginning and end of each data character (start and stop bits) to synchronize the sending and receiving devices. Commonly used with modems on PCs and minicomputers.

ATTENUATION: Attenuation refers to an undesirable condition in which the message signals sent along a channel are corrupted as a consequence of the waveform of the signal being chopped off. Attenuation is related to the transmission medium used in the link and to the frequency of the message signal. Usually, the attenuation attributed to any component of a system is measured in decibels. Normally, repeaters are used to overcome the effects of attenuation.

BACKBONE: The trunk system used by a multimedia LAN to connect various subnetworks, generally at high data rates over enterprise-wide distances.

BANDWIDTH: The information-carrying capacity of a channel; it is measured in hertz (Hz). The bandwidth is the difference between the highest and lowest frequencies that can be used on the channel.

BASEBAND: The frequency range in which a signal is actually generated, as opposed to the frequencies that might be used to transmit the signal after modulation.

BASEBAND SIGNALING: A data transmission technique in which only one signal occupies a cable at a time. Many office-oriented LANs employ baseband signaling techniques.

BAUD: A measure of signaling speed on a network commonly confused with bits per second. Baud refers to the number of symbols that can be transferred in 1 s, no matter how many bits are represented by each symbol.

BIT: The basic unit of information used in computers and digital communications.

BLOCK: A block is a group of characters, bits, or words transmitted as a unit of data in a system.

BRANCHING TREE TOPOLOGY: The topology that results from interconnecting the nodes of a system in a geographically hierarchical manner. For example, one node may interconnect to distinct branches of the tree. On each branch one node may interconnect several smaller branches.

BRIDGE: Software and hardware used to connect two LANs using the same logical link control but possibly different medium access controls.

BROADBAND: Communications that take advantage of a transmission medium known as frequency division multiplexing (FDM) to divide a single channel into a number of smaller, independent frequency channels. The resultant wide bandwidth allows more bits per unit of time to be moved from point to point, and can be used to transfer voice, data, and video.

BROADBAND SIGNALING: A data transmission technique that permits simultaneous transmission of multiple signals over a single cable at different frequencies. Braodband LANs can carry video, radio, and other signals, in addition to data.

BUS: Data transmission and wiring scheme (like Ethernet) in which all workstations simultaneously receive a data broadcast. Broadband networks use a variant of bus topology known as *tree* topology, in which all network branches radiate out from a common point known as the headend.

CABLE: A group of conductive elements, such as wires, or other media, such as fiber optics, packaged as a single line to interconnect communications systems.

CACHE: Extra RAM in server used to hold data requested by workstations; helps data requests execute more quickly.

CARRIER SENSE MULTIPLE ACCESS (CSMA): A mechanism for accessing a broadcast communication medium which tries to avoid transmission collision by not transmitting if there is already a transmission in progress. The presence of another transmission is detected by sensing the carrier of the transmission.

CENTRALIZED NETWORK: A computer network with a central processing node through which all data and communications flow.

CHANNEL: On broadband networks, a channel is a 6-MHz-wide frequency band corresponding to a single TV channel.

CHANNEL CAPACITY: The maximum number of 6-MHz channels a broadband network can carry.

CHEAPERNET: An IEEE 802.3 standard for lower-cost contention access bus networks using less expensive coaxial cabling.

CIRCUIT: The electrical path between two endpoints over which one-way or two-way communications can be provided.

CIRCUIT SWITCHING: A method of communicating in which a dedicated communications path is established between two devices through one or more intermediate switching nodes. Unlike packet switching, digital data are sent as a continuous stream of bits. Bandwidth is guaranteed, and delay is essentially limited to propagation time. The telephone system uses circuit switching.

CLUSTER: A cluster refers to a concentration of devices at a specified point in the network such as two or more data terminals linked to a concentrator which determines their interface to other terminal devices over a communications channel.

COAXIAL CABLE: Network wiring media; varies in thickness depending on transmission requirements. Signals transmit on inner copper conductor which is packaged in plastic insulation. The insulation is encased with a foil or copper shield.

COMMUNICATION SERVER: A network node that serves as a gateway to external computer systems and networks. A communications server may be configured with modems, bisynchronous communications adapters, or other components.

CONCENTRATOR: In local area networks employing a star topology, the central hub to which network nodes are connected.

CONNECTIVITY: In a local area network, the ability of any device attached to the distribution system to establish a session with any other device.:
DLC: Data Link Control; IBM's SNA protocol layer that controls data transmission, error detection, and error recovery between two nodes.

DATA LINK LAYER: Second level in OSI Reference Model. Controls data flow in and out of each network device.

DATA RATE: Data rate is a term used to describe the speed at which devices or circuits operate when handling digital information.

DEDICATED SERVER: A network computer that operates exclusively as a server--that is, it exists solely to provide resources to other network nodes. A dedicated server cannot be used as a workstation. Some network operating systems require dedicated servers.

DISK SERVER: A network node that provides shared access to a magnetic disk drive or an optical disk drive; sometimes termed a "file server."

DISTRIBUTED NETWORK: A network configuration in which all node pairs are connected either directly, or through redundant paths through intermediate nodes.

DUPLEX: A type of transmission that affords simultaneous operation in both directions.

ELECTRONIC MAIL: Electronic mail is a systsem offering person-to-person communication of messages utilizing electronic mechanisms for entry, delivery, and transmission of information in a visual form.

ETHERNET: Popular network wiring and signaling protocol. Uses CSMA/CD.

FDDI: Fiber distributed data interface, a new proposed standard for token-passing ring topology, fiber optic LANs operating at 100 Mb/s.

FIBER-OPTIC CABLE: Glass or plastic cable that carries data sent via light impulses. Can allow very high bandwidth, for example, in excess of 3 GHz, with very low error rates. Fiber optics are not subject to electrical or electromagnetic interference.

FILE SERVER: Network computer that stores and manages files in shared or private subdirectories.

FILE SHARING: The process whereby a given data file is accessible to multiple network nodes for entry, modification, or retrieval as authorized. Network nodes that maintain such shared files are termed file servers.

FRAME: Token Ring network data packet.

GATEWAY: Hardware and software that lets users on a network access resources on a different, incompatible network.

HALF DUPLEX: Half duplex refers to a transmission channel in which two-way transmission is possible but only one way at a time.

HEADEND: The physical location as well as the equipment used at the base of a broadband system. Headend equipment can include satellite reception or transmission gear, antennas, preamplifiers, demodulators and modulators, signal processors, character generators and TV cameras, status monitoring computers and software, network management consoles, bridges, routers, and gateways.

HOST: A network computer that provides network services like printing and file sharing. Mainframe and minicomputers are traditionally called hosts, serving the needs of users who link to them via dumb terminals and PCs.

INTERNETWORKING: Communication among devices across multiple networks.

IPX: Internetwork Protocol Exchange; Novell's implementation of XNS protocols in Netware.

ISO: International Standards Organization is an international body including standard groups from nations around the world which develops standards for goods and services which facilitate international exchange and trade. Developed the OSI Reference Model.

LOCAL AREA NETWORK (LAN): A privately owned communications network operating at high speed over relatively small distances and linking computers, peripherals, and other devices.

LOCKING: Method of protecting the integrity of shared data on a LAN. A multiuser database uses record-locking to prevent more than one user from concurrently using the same record.

LU 6.2. (Logical Unit 6.2): Logical Units are IBM's network-defined paths to computers or devices like printers. LU 6.2 is the Logical Unit type that implements IBM APPC peer-to-peer (or device-to-device) networking scheme under SNA.

MANAGER'S WORKSTATION: A microcomputer containing an integrated package of software designed to improve the productivity of managers. A workstation will usually, though not exclusively, include a word processor, a spreadsheet program, a communications program, and a data manager.

MEDIA ACCESS CONTROL (MAC): Controls LAN traffic to help avoid data collisions as packets move on and off the network through the adapter card; a subset of the OSI Data Link Layer.

MEGABITS PER SECOND (MBPS): A measure of channel capacity in terms of data rate; a common unit of measurement in present-day systems.

METROPOLITAN AREA NETWORK (MAN): A network having a diameter of not more than 50 km.

MODEM (MOdulator/DEModulator): A hardware device that permits computers and terminals to communicate with each other using analog circuits such as telephone lines. The modem's modulator translates the digital computer signals into analog signals that can be transmitted over a telephone line. The modem's demodulator converts analog signals into digital signals for the computer's use.

MULTIPLEXER: A multiplexer is a device enabling a number of message signals to share the same physical transmission channel by utilizing the techniques of time division multiplexing (TDM) or frequency division multiplexing (FDM).

NETBIOS: Network Basic Input/Output System; IBM/Sytek-developed software used to link hardware with the NOS or to open Session Layer communications.

NETWORK: An interconnected and coordinated system of geographically dispersed communications devices (terminals) connected so that signal transmission to or among any of the devices is practical and reliable. The computers can send and receive data among themselves and share certain devices such as hard disks and printers.

NETWORK ARCHITECTURE: Network architecture is a definition of the functions, protocol, and logical components of a network and how they should act.

NETWORK INTERFACE CARD (NIC): Hardware used to physically link a workstation to a LAN's wiring media. Firmware and software complete link to the NOS.

NETWORK LAYER: Third level in OSI Reference Model. Its switching and routing rules are key to the operation of large internetworks.

NETWORK OPERATING SYSTEM: A set of control programs designed to manage local area network resources and activities.

NFS: Network File System, a distributed file and peripheral sharing protocol developed by Sun Microsystems.

NODE: An identifiable point in a design that must be electrically connected to other nodes. A node may or may not be associated with a specific device or topology.

NOISE: The extra signals that are always received on a circuit that can cause errors in the received information.

NOS: Network Operating System; system software that creates the network and controls who can use it and how. It can be server-based or peer-to-peer (where every node can be a server of sorts).

OPERATING SYSTEM: The basic software that drives the hardware, that is, the resource management programs: monitor routines, input/output control, allocation capabilities, interrupt processing, swapping in central memory, job scheduling, and management of peripherals. The kernel of any computer.

OPTICAL FIBERS: Optical fibers offer a bounded transmission medium along which data is carried as pulses of light.

OSI: Open Systems Interconnection Reference Model. ISO's scheme for standardizing all aspects of network operations and management, communications, and applications. Consists of seven layers:

> 7. Application
> 6. Presentation
> 5. Session
> 4. Transport
> 3. Network
> 2. Data Link
> 1. Physical

PACKET: A group of information transmitted over a network. Each packet includes addressing and control data.

PACKET SWITCHING: The process of transmitting packets of data from sender to receiver where the transmission channel is occupied only for the period of time while the packet is being transmitted.

PEER-TO-PEER NETWORK: Decentralized NOS that lets workstations share and use resources on other workstations while running local applications. It differs from a centralized NOS where workstations can use resources only on the server. A peer-to-peer NOS usually is RAM-based software that runs on every workstation.

PHYSICAL LAYER: First level in OSI Reference Model; governs physical network connection of workstations to the wiring media.

POINT-TO-POINT CONNECTION: A connection between two entities without the intervention of an intermediate device.:

POLLING: The sequential process of inviting entities to transmit data.

PRESENTATION LAYER: Sixth level in OSI Reference Model; reformats differences in user data into a form usable by the network's Application Layer.

PRINT SERVER: A networked computer that lets other workstations print to its attached printers.

PROTOCOL: A set of rules that govern communication between computers. Such rules apply to data format, transmission timing and sequencing, and error handling.

REDIRECTOR: Software that captures workstation application requests for services like printing and sends them to network devices.

REMOTE FILE SERVICE (RFS): Distributed file system like Sun Microsystem's NFS that lets workstations use remote resources as if they were local.

REPEATER: Hardware and software required to join two LAN segments using the same protocols but possibly different physical media. On a broadband LAN, repeaters are called amplifiers. Repeaters operate at the physical layer of the open systems interconnection (OSI) protocol suite.

ROUTER: Hardware and software used to connect two LANs that have the same network architecture through the first three levels of the OSI model.

SAA: IBM's Systems Application Architecture; specifications for programmers to create a similar look and feel for applications on mainframes, minicomputers, and PCs.

SERVER: Any networked computer that provides things like file, print, or mail services. A term sometimes applied to a primary file-sharing computer running a centralized network operating system like Netware or 3+Open.

SESSION LAYER: Fifth level in OSI Reference Model; used for administrative tasks like security.

SMB: Server Message Block; a distributed file system that lets workstations use remote devices, files, and applications as if they were local. LAN Manager uses SMB at a very low level.

SNA: IBM's System Network Architecture, a network model that provides specifications in a manner like the OSI Reference Model.

STAR: A network topology consisting of one central node with point-to-point links to several other nodes. Control of the network is usually located in the central node or switch, with all routing of network message traffic performed by the central node.

STARLAN: An AT&T-developed CSMA network system used on twisted-pair telephone wire.

SYNCHRONOUS TRANSMISSION: 1. A method of high speed transmission in which the timing of each bit of data is precisely controlled. 2. Communications in which there is a constant time between successive bits, characters, or events. The timing is achieved by synchronizing the clocking of data transmission.

T-1: Digital transmission scheme that sends data at 1.544 megabits per second. T-1 circuits can carry 24 simultaneous 64-kbps channels. They often serve as wide area network backbones. Some network operating system vendors now sell gateways to link to T-1 circuits. National T-1 connections can be rented from telephone companies.

TAP: A device that allows an exit from a main line of a communications system.

TCP/IP: Transmission Control Protocol/Internet Protocol; Transport and Network Layer protocols developed by the Department of Defense. Primarily used for linking different computers on large networks. Often used to link PCs with Unix hosts.

TOKEN BUS: A medium access control technique for bus/tree. Stations form a logical ring, around which a token is passed. A station receiving the token may transmit data, and then must pass the token on to the next station in the ring.

TOKEN PASSING: A network data-access method; computers wait to get control of a "token" that lets them send data.

TOKEN RING: A LAN ring wiring topology that uses token passing for data access; based on the IEEE 802.5 standard.

TOPOLOGY: The physical layout and architecture of a local area network. Common topologies are the bus, tree, star, and ring. Wide area networks use a mesh topology.

TRANSPORT LAYER: Fourth level of OSI Reference Model; provides error checking and routing of data packets.

TREE: A topology in which stations are attached to a shared transmission medium. The transmission medium is a branching cable emanating from a headend, with no closed circuits. Transmissions propagate throughout all branches of the tree, and are received by all stations.

TWISTED PAIR WIRE: Two thin wires twisted around each other to create cable for linking things like telephones, PBXs, computers, and terminals; it sometimes has extra shielding. Its low cost and easy installation make it a very popular media for wiring LANs.

WIRING CLOSET: A room or other location at a facility where network wiring is concentrated for attachment to devices. Wiring closets sometimes are used as repeater or hub sites.

WORKSTATION: A location at which an individual works; generally used to denote electronic, usually computer-linked, devices which an individual uses in the course of his/her job, in an automated office setting.

X.25: Standard for linking computers to packet-switched networks like Telenet and Tymnet.

X.400: Developing standard for electronic-mail addressing.

XNS: Xerox Network Services; another distributed file system that lets workstations use remote resources as if they were local.

References to Glossary

Cheong, V.E., and R. A. Hirschheim. *Local Area Networks: Issues, Products, and Developments.* Chichester, England: John Wiley & Sons, 1983.

Chorafas, Dimitris N. *Designing and Implementing Local Area Networks.* New York: McGraw-Hill, 1984.

Cole, Robert. *Computer Communications.* 2nd ed. New York: Macmillan, 1986.

Kemper, Marlyn. *Networking: Choosing a LAN Path to Interconnection.* Metuchen, N.J.: Scarecrow Press, 1987.

Kim, Gary Y. *Broadband LAN Technology.* Norwood, Mass.: Artech House, 1988.

Saffady, William. "Local Area Networks: A Survey of the Technology." *Library Technology Reports* Vol. 26, no. 1 (January-February 1990).

Stallings, William. *Local Networks: An Introduction.* New York: Macmillan Publishing Company, 1984.

Weidlin, James R., and Thomas B. Cross. *Networking Personal Computers in Organizations.* Homewood, Ill.: Dow Jones-Irwin, 1986.

Bibliography

Books

Archer, Rowland. *The Practical Buide to Local Area Networks.* Berkeley, Calif.: Osborne McGraw-Hill, 1986.

Belitos, Byron and Jay Misra. *Business Telematics: Corporate Networks for the Information Age.* Homewood, Ill.: Dow Jones-Irwin, 1986.

Black, Uyless. *Computer Networks: Protocols, Standards, and Interfaces.* Englewood Cliffs, N.J.: Prentice-Hall, 1987.

Brumm, Penn. *The Micro to Mainframe Connection.* Blue Ridge Summit, Penn.: Tab Books, 1986.

Cheong, V. E. and R. A. Hirschheim. *Local Area Networks: Issues, Products, and Developments.* Chichester, England: John Wiley & Sons, 1983.

Chorafas, Dimitris N. *Designing and Implementing Local Area Networks.* New York: McGraw-Hill, 1984.

Culotta, Wendy, Zorana Ercegovac, and Dana Roth. *Local Area Networks and Libraries: The Los Angeles Chapter of ASIS Seminar Proceedings.* Studio City, Calif.: Pacific Information, Inc., 1985.

Currie, W. Scott. *LANs Explained: A Guide to Local Area Networks.* New York: Halsted Press, 1988.

Davis, George R., ed. *The Local Area Network Handbook.* New York: McGraw Hill Publishers, 1984.

Digital Equipment Corporation. *Introduction to Local Area Networks.* Maynard, Mass.: Digital Equipment Corporation, 1982.

Durr, Michael and Mark Gibbs. *Networking Personal Computers.* Carmel, Ind.: Cue Corporation, 1989.

Fortier, Paul J. *Handbook of LAN Technology.* New York: Intertext Publications, McGraw Hill, 1989.

Fritz, James S., Charles F. Kaldenbach, and Louis M. Progar. *Local Area Networks: Selection Guidelines.* Englewood Cliffs, N.J.: Prentice-Hall, Inc., 1985.

Gee, K.C.E. *Local Area Networks.* Manchester, England: The National Computing Centre Limited, 1982.

Green, James Harry. *Local Area Networks: A User's Guide for Business Professionals.* Glenview, Ill.: Scott, Foresman and Company, 1985.

Hancock, Bill. *Designing and Implementing Ethernet Networks.* Wellesley, Mass.: QED Information Sciences, Inc., 1988.

Helal, Ahmed H. *Local Library Systems.* Essen, West Germany: Essen University Library, 1984.

Hopper, Andrew, Steven Temple, and Robin Williamson. *Local Area Network Design.* Wokingham, England: Addison-Wesley Publishing Co., 1986.

Hordeski, Michael F. *Microcomputer LANs: Network Design and Implmentation.* Blue Ridge Summit, Penn.: TAB Professional and Reference Books, 1987.

Kemper, Marlyn. "Local Area Networking: The Management Problem." In *The Library Microcomputer Environment: Management Issues,* by Sheila S. Intner and Jane Anne Hannigan, 187-206. New York: Oryx Press, 1988.

_____. *Networking: Choosing a LAN Path to Interconnection.* Metuchen, N.J.: Scarecrow Press, 1987

Kim, Gary Y. *Broadband Lan Technology.* Norwood, Mass.: Artech House, Inc., 1988.

Kleeman, Michael, et al. *PC LAN Primer.* Indianapolis, Ind.: Howard W. Sams & Co., 1987.

Lefkon, Richard G. *Selecting a Local Area Network*. New York: American Management Association, 1986.

Madron, Thomas W. *Local Area Networks: The Second Generation*. New York: Wiley & Sons, 1988.

Mathov, Mauricio J. "How to Select a LAN." In *Information Network and Data Communication, 1. Proceedings of the IFIPTC6 International Conference on Information Network and Data Communication*, by Dipak Khakhar, 99-108. Ronneby Brunn, Sweden, 11-14 May, 1986. Amsterdam: North Holland, 1987.

Nemzow, Martin A. W. *Keeping the Link: Ethernet Installation and Management*. New York: McGraw-Hill, 1988.

Novell. *Netware Buyer's Guide*. Provo, Utah: Novell, Inc., 1989.

Schatt, Stan. *Understanding Local Area Networks*. Indianapolis, Ind.: Howard W. Sams & Co., 1988.

Stallings, William. *Local Networks: An Introduction*. New York: Macmillan Publishing Company, 1984.

Tangney, Brendan, and Donal O'Mahony. *Local Area Networks and their Applications*. Englewood Cliffs, N.J.: Prentice Hall, 1988.

Weidlein, James R. and Thomas B. Cross. *Networking Personal Computers in Organizations*. Homewood, Ill.: Dow Jones-Irwin, 1986.

Journals

Adams, Roy J., and Mel Collier. "Local area network development at Leicester Polytechnic Library." *Program: Automated Library and Information Systems* 21, no.3 (July 1987): 273-282.

Allen-Tonar, Larry. "Networked Computers Attract Security Problems, Abuse." *Networking Management* 7, no.12 (December 1989): 48-53.

Angier, J. J., and S. B. Hoehl. "Local Area Networks (LAN) in the Special Library. Part 1--A Planning Model." *Online* 10, no.6 (November 1986): 19-28.

Angus, Jeff. "How to Work with Network Consultants." *InfoWorld* 11, no.15, Target Edition no.8 (April 10, 1989): S1-4.

Antonell, Laurie. "Changing Environment Complicates Network Manager's Job." *LAN Times* (December 1988): 19.

Baird, Patricia M., and Beatrice Borer. "An Experiment in Computer Conferencing using a Local Area Network." *The Electronic Library* 5, no.3 (June 1987): 162-169.

Barker, Ralph. "The Lady or the Tiger." *InfoWorld* 11, no.17, Target Edition no.10 (April 24, 1989): S1-3.

Beiser, Karl. "Lantastic Z." *CD-ROM End User* 2, no.1 (May 1990): 82-84.

Bohm, Victoria. "Gaining Control of LANs for WAN Integration." *Networking Management* 8, no.9 (September 1990): 62-66.

Brenner, Aaron. "Client-Server Computing Has the Advantage." *InfoWorld* 11, no.15 (April 10, 1989): 12.

Brown, Ray. "Some Optical Illusions aren't Illusions." *LAN Times* (June 1988): 54-57+.

Buerger, David J. "Computer Security Issues Now Front Page News." *InfoWorld* 11, no.2, Target Edition no.1 (January 9, 1989): S1-3.

_____. "Expanding Network Horizons Using Wide Area Networks." *InfoWorld* 11, no.19, Target Edition no.12 (May 8, 1989): S1-12.

_____. "Myth and Reality: Pitfalls in LAN Cost Justification." *InfoWorld* 11, no.10, Target Edition no.5 (March 6, 1989): S1-4.

_____, Tracey Capen, and Mary O'Donnell. "Move Over Netware?" *InfoWorld* 11, no.29 (July 17, 1989): 49-59.

Caswell, Stephen A. "The New Mail." *InfoWorld* 11, no.39, Target Edition no.30 (September 25, 1989): S1-4.

Caton, Michael. "Protecting PCs from Sags and Dips, Surges and Spikes." *PC Week* 7, no. 36 (September 10, 1990): 127.

Cesar, Tom N. "Careful Planning Helps Keep Network Costs Down." *InfoWorld* 11, no.21, Target Edition no.14 (May 22, 1989): S14.

Collier, Mel, and David Piper. "Multi-site library networking: experience of the Polytechnic of Central London." *Program: Automated Library and Information Systems* 18, no.2 (April 1984): 147-156.

Copeland, Joyce M., and Stephen Flood. "Applications of local area networks in special libraries and information services; research in progress." *Program: Automated Library and Information Systems* 19, no.1 (January 1985): 72-76.

_____. "Users and Local Area Networks: Opportunities for Information Transfer." *The Electronic Library* 2, no.4 (October 1984): 273-277.

Crabb, Don. "A Glance at LAN Server Operating Systems." *InfoWorld* 11, no.48, Target Edition no.38 (November 27, 1989): S4.

_____. "Administering a Networked Society: Rules to Compute By." *InfoWorld* 12, no.11, Target Edition no.10 (March 12, 1990): S9.

_____. "Backing Up is Hard To Do." *InfoWorld* 12, no.7, Target Edition no.6 (February 12, 1990): S1-8.

_____. "Extending Your Network's Reach: Repeaters, Bridges, Routers, Brouters, and Gateways." *InfoWorld* 11, no.26, Target Edition no.18 (June 26, 1989): 1-4.

_____. "Planning a LAN Database." *InfoWorld* 12, no.24, Target Edition no.17 (June 11, 1990): S1-S4.

Currid, Cheryl. "Getting Simple Things Right Paves Way for Downsizing." *PC Week* 7, no.16 (April 23, 1990): 115.

Currid, Cheryl C. "Planning, Designing and Staffing LANs." *Networking Management* 8, no.3 (March 1990): 61-64.

Dortch, Michael. "Tripping the Light Fantastic." *LAN Times* 6, no.8 (August 1989): 81-82.

Eskow, Dennis. "Users Shed LAN Drudgery, Keep their Data." *PC Week* 7, no.6 (February 12, 1990): 1.

"Farming Off the File Server." *LAN Times* (April 1988): 44-47.

Farr, Rick C. "LANs: A New Technology to Improve Library Automation." *Drexel Library Quarterly* 20, no.4 (Fall 1984): 56-63.

Fisher, Sharon. "Future of Fax Machines is Very Bright (and Diverse) Indeed." *InfoWorld* 12, no.9, Target Edition no.8 (February 26, 1990): S8-9.

_____. "The Future of Networks." *InfoWorld* 12, no.23, Target Edition no.16 (June 4, 1990): S1-S3.

Frank, Howard. "Dealing with Networks in the Read World." *Networking Management* 8, no.2 (February 1990): 33-34.

Gantz, John. "LAN Servers: Upwardly Mobile Path for Personal Computers." *InfoWorld* 12, no.21 (May 21, 1990): 46.

Glass, Brett. "Fiber in Your Future." *InfoWorld* 11, no.41, Target Edition no.32 (October 9, 1989): S1-4.

_____. "Netbios: The Most Misunderstood LAN Interface." *InfoWorld* 12, no.16, Target Edition no.13 (April 16, 1990): S15-16.

_____. "'Smart Hubs' Handle Network Problems." *InfoWorld* 11, no.28, Target Edition no.20 (July 10, 1989): S14.

_____. "Spread-Spectrum Packet Radio Made Accessible." *InfoWorld* 12, no.18, Target Edition no.14 (April 30, 1990): S3.

_____. "Understanding the OSI Reference Model Standard." *InfoWorld* 12, no.16, Target Edition no.13 (April 16, 1990): S12-14.

_____. "X.25 Useful for Global WAN's, E-Mail." *InfoWorld* 11, no.26, Target Edition no.18 (June 26, 1989): S7.

_____, and Raphael Needleman. "Network Fax Servers: New Products Deliver the Message." *InfoWorld* 12, no.9, Target Edition no.8 (February 26, 1990): S1-6+.

Henderson, Tom. "Tips for Network Installers." *LAN Times* (December 1987): 20.

Howard, Stephen. "Closing the Gap Between Theory and User Needs." *Networking Management* 7, no.12 (December 1989): 56-61.

Hume, Barbara R. "Broadband and Baseband: Two Kinds of LANs." *LAN Times* (August 1987): 10-11.

Hurwicz, Mike. "A New Twist on Ethernet." *LAN Times* (June 1988): 51-52+.

_____. "Premises Cabling: Managing a Thorny Thicket." *Networking Management* 7, no.11 (November 1989): 62-68.

_____. "Securing the LAN." *LAN Times* (August 1987): 35-58.

_____. "The Writing on the Wall." *LAN Times* (May 1988): 41-42+.

Kerry, Nina B. "FAX Networks Offer Users Advanced Capabilities." *Networking Management* 8, no.3 (March 1990): 41-46.

Kidwell, Mary Coyle. "An Integrated Online Library System as a Node in a Local Area Network: The Mitre Experience." *The Electronic Library* 5, no.6 (December 1987): 342-346.

Kiesler, Sara. "Bridging the Gap: E-Mail Brings Out the Best-and Worst-in Group Interaction." *InfoWorld* 11, no.35, Target Edition no.26 (August 28, 1989): S4-7.

Krumm, Rob. "Learning to Data Share: Making the Switch to Using Your Programs on a Multiuser LAN." *InfoWorld* 12, no.4, Target Edition no.4 (January 1990): S1-6.

_____. "Networks Without Servers: Alternatives to the Traditional LAN." *InfoWorld* 11, no.21, Target Edition no.14 (May 22, 1989): S1-10.

"LAN Architecture: File Server vs. Client/Server." *InfoWorld* 12, no.24, Target Edition no.17 (June 11, 1990): S8-S9.

Learn, Larry L. "NETWORKS: A Review of their Technology, Architecture and Implementation." *Library Hi Tech* 6, no.2 (1988): 19-49.

Levert, Virginia M. "Applications of Local Area Networks of Microcomputers in Libraries." *Information Technology and Libraries* 4, no.1 (March 1985): 9-18.

"Local Area Networks (LAN) in the Special Library. Part 2--Implementation." *Online* 10, no.6 (November 1986): 29-36.

McQueen, Howard. "Considering a CD-ROM Network?" *CD-ROM End User* 1, no.12 (April 1990): 61-63.

_____. "Minimizing Ongoing Operating Costs." *CD-ROM End User* 2, no.2 (June 1990): 34-36.

_____. "Networking CD-ROMs" *CD-ROM End User* 1, no.11 (March 1990): 92-95.

Mandelbaum, Jane B. "READS: A Networked PC System." *Information Technology and Libraries* 8, no.2 (June 1989): 196-202.

Needleman, Raphael. "Server-Based and Peer-to-Peer LAN Designs." *InfoWorld* 11, no.46, Target Edition no.36 (November 13, 1989): S20-23.

_____. "The Other Side: A Unix Vendor Looks at the PC LAN Market." *InfoWorld* 11, no.17, Target Edition no.10 (April 24, 1989): S4.

Nickerson, Gord. "Installing a Low-Cost CD-ROM Network." *CD-ROM End User* 2, no.2 (June 1990): 26-29.

"NICs: the Nerves of a LAN." *LAN Times* (April 1988): 58.

Novak, Stewart. "Protecting the Network Against Power Problems." *Networking Management* 8, no.8 (August 1990): 62-66.

Parker, Rachel. "Behind the Screens: Network Change the Way Worker Communicate." *InfoWorld* 11, no.35, Target Edition no.26 (August 28, 1989): S1-7.

"PCs-on-a-Card Give Remote LAN Access." *PC Week* 7, no.13 (April 2, 1990): 73-76.

Powell, Dave. "Network Abuse: Who's the Enemy?" *Networking Management* 8, no.9 (September 1990): 27-34.

Raymond, Chadwick, and Charles Anderson. "Local Area Networks: Reaping the Benefits." *Wilson Library Bulletin* 62, no.3 (November 1987): 21-24.

Saffady, William. "Local Area Networks: A Survey of the Technology." *Library Technology Reports* 26, no. 1 (January-February 1990).

Snapp, Cheryl. "Getting from Point A to Point B." *LAN Times* 6, no.8 (August 1989): 66-68.

Stephens, Mark. "Bus, Star, Ring Topologies Increase Network Options." *InfoWorld* 11, no.2 (January 9, 1989): 12.

_____. "MAC-Layer LAN Bridges Don't Need to Stand on Protocol." *InfoWorld* 11, no.24 (June 12, 1989): 18.

_____. "Studies Reveal the Hidden Costs for Installing, Maintaining LANs." *InfoWorld* 11, no.38 (September 18, 1989): 37.

_____. "3 Devices Solve Traffic Problems." *InfoWorld* 11, no.22 (May 29, 1989): 14.

_____. "Wired: How PC Networks Are Changing the Way We Work." *InfoWorld* 11, no.13 (March 27, 1989): 41-46.

Stephenson, Peter, David Buerger, Raphael Needleman. "Managing Your LAN: a Balance of Many Skills." *InfoWorld* 11, no.6, Target Edition no.3 (February 6, 1989): S1-6.

"Tracking Down the Soft, Soft Costs of LANs." *LAN Times* (December 1987): 17-18.

Waters, Sandy. "15 Questions to Ask Before You Buy Your LAN." *InfoWorld* 11, no.30, Target Edition no.22 (July 24, 1989): S7-8.

Wylie, Margie. "Choosing a LAN File Server." *InfoWorld* 12, no.11, Target Edition no.10 (March 12, 1990): S1-3.

Technical Manuals

NOVELL Technical Manuals, June 1990 Edition. Manual Revision 1.01 (For netware 386 v3.1). Provo, Utah: NOVELL Inc.

Index